Computer
Security

COVER

A computer, rendered as a one and a
zero to symbolize the digital nature of
the machine, stands secure behind a
protective brick wall.

UNDERSTANDING COMPUTERS

Computer
Security

BY THE EDITORS OF TIME-LIFE BOOKS

TIME-LIFE BOOKS, ALEXANDRIA, VIRGINIA

Contents

The Information Society at Risk

Companies that manage their payrolls by computer increasingly offer employees the option of having their paychecks deposited directly into a bank account, instead of receiving a printed check and banking it personally. While many workers gratefully accept the service, others mistrust it; they would rather have the money in hand. Perhaps the doubters are simply old-fashioned and prefer the traditional way of being paid. Whatever their reason, they may have a case.

The money is deposited by a telephone message between computers, one instructing another to subtract the sum from the company's account and to add it to the employee's balance. Coded for brevity, the message may be only a line or two and take less than a second to transmit. Depending on how far the message must travel, it is likely to go part of the way along telephone cables and part as a radio signal beamed between microwave-relay towers or even bounced from a communications satellite in orbit 22,240 miles above the earth.

From start to finish, it is a trip fraught with potential hazards. At either end, someone might accidentally garble the message so that too little money is sent or the correct amount goes to the wrong account. A breakdown in the system could occur, convincing the originator of the message that it had been received when it had never been sent. The sequence of messages that make up an entire payroll— or an even larger portion of the hundreds of billions of dollars that change hands electronically each day in the United States—might be intercepted along the way, allowing the eavesdropper at a single stroke to divert a king's ransom to an unauthorized account.

To be sure, traditional payroll methods are vulnerable, too. A light-fingered thief might steal a check from someone's pocket, or a well-organized band of robbers could highjack the armored truck that delivers a cash payroll. But unlike a purloined check, which is soon missed, or the commotion of an armored-truck job, which instantly galvanizes the police, a computer heist occurs silently, at nearly the speed of light. It might go undiscovered for several days, time enough for a clever crook to make a clean getaway. An employee might not know the electronic paycheck is missing until irate phone calls begin coming in from creditors and checks return from the bank marked "INSUFFICIENT FUNDS."

The transfer of vast wealth by computer is certainly reason enough for those in charge of these systems to see that they function as they are supposed to and that they are secure from internal and external assault. But even more is at stake. Credit-rating information, including credit-card numbers, is stored in computers and passed among those with a legitimate need for the information, in much the same way that a payroll is distributed. A credit-card number in the wrong hands, whether intercepted in transmission or plucked directly from the computer where it is stored, is an invitation to fraud. Though the cardholder may be held responsible for only a small fraction of the unexpected purchases that appear on the bill, in the end the public pays, as credit-card companies raise fees to compensate for the losses.

Barriers to keep outsiders away from a computer and its data provide a partial measure of security. Equally important is safeguarding the system and its contents against subversion from within.

7

All manner of confidential data, from medical records to the names and addresses of advertisers in the personal column of classifieds, are entrusted to computers. Businesses use computers to store trade secrets that, if stolen by competitors, could lead to bankruptcy. Lawyers store the confidences of their clients in them. Libraries catalogue collections with them. Nations conduct sensitive diplomacy through them and keep secret military plans in them.

Moreover, the flow of daily life depends on computers running without a hitch. They are used to switch electric power from areas that have a surplus to sectors where demand exceeds supply. They coordinate the flow of transcontinental telephone communications. Other computers function in roles where the price of failure or disruption could be catastrophe—the regulation of life-support systems in hospitals, for example, or monitoring of nuclear reactors.

A HOST OF THREATS

From time to time, when computers fail to perform as the world has grown to expect them to, a great hue and cry ensues. But the real wonder is that the remarkable machines function as reliably as they do. Physical hazards abound. Should a careless nudge of an elbow, for example, send a flood of coffee across a desk toward a personal computer, not only the computer is endangered: A magnetic disk used with such computers for storing data could be inundated, and the disk's coffee-coated surface might never again yield up the information entrusted to it. Skin oil and dirt from a fingerprint can have equally unfortunate results on a disk.

A sudden surge or momentary lapse in a computer's electrical power supply is as capable of erasing or scrambling data as the clumsiest data-processing employee or most malicious vandal. Military planners ponder the effects of nuclear explosions on computers and other electronic equipment. Their chief concern is not blast, heat or radiation—usually considered the most devastating forces unleashed by such an explosion—but something called electromagnetic pulse, or EMP. When an atomic or hydrogen bomb detonates, it emits a burst of radiation that interacts with the earth's magnetic field to create a powerful surge of electromagnetic energy. This pulse can induce in the fine web of a computer's circuitry an electrical current strong enough to bring the device to a stop or even destroy it. In that event, missiles could stray off course, aircraft could crash and vital communications could be disrupted.

The human caretakers and taskmasters of computer systems can cause as much harm as any physical hazard. In some instances, these trusted insiders steal or do other deliberate mischief. But more often they make simple mistakes that, taken together, are fully as damaging as crime. "Security seems to be always directed against willful and malicious activities," notes Harry DeMaio, the director of security for International Business Machines, Inc.—yet carelessness is an even larger problem. The inconvenience and financial loss caused by errors and omissions far exceed the toll exacted by crime. For example, lack of diligence in making backup copies of data can transform the annoyance of mistakenly erasing the original into a costly nightmare.

Nonetheless, the most colorful—if not the most destructive—collection of computer nemeses are not professionals who work with computers every day, but youthful amateurs who experiment at night. They are the hackers.

8

That it would be possible one day for even children to violate computers and the information they contain had been foretold by security specialists, who saw that the characteristics that make computers useful and powerful tools also make them attractive and vulnerable targets. Information once stored on paper at scattered locations is now concentrated in large computer data bases and dispersed electronically. Even the speed of computers is a liability: A machine that retrieves facts quickly can also be used to steal facts at a phenomenal rate.

In 1984, editors of *IEEE Spectrum,* a publication of the International Electrical and Electronics Engineers, published an examination of computer security. "Twenty years ago," they wrote, "anyone who committed a crime that involved a computer was probably employed by a data-processing facility." At that time, only government agencies and large corporations had computers, which were run solely by authorized operators. Companies with excess computer capacity sold it to others in an arrangement called time sharing, which allowed organizations not rich enough to own computers to share in the benefits. Within a few years, hundreds of subscribers began communicating great distances with computers over telephone lines specially laid at tremendous cost. To prevent theft of valuable data-processing time by outsiders, subscribers used passwords—secret sequences of letters and numbers—to identify themselves to the computer. But passwords were often compromised, and their illicit use caused legitimate customers to be billed for services they never received.

NETWORK VULNERABILITY

As computers proliferated and companies who owned them wanted their employees to have access to the expensive hardware from a distance, public networks using regular telephone lines to transfer data between computers emerged as an economical substitute for private telephone lines, compounding the security problem. By the 1980s, the IEEE editors continued, "an unauthorized user who had obtained a valid password could get into the computer systems—for profit or for fun—from anywhere in the country."

Even as computers and their lines of communications grew more vulnerable to attack, engineers provided two instruments necessary for youngsters to intrude on them. One is the inexpensive personal computer, the other a device called a modulator/demodulator, or modem, that converts computer data into signals for transmission over telephone lines. Almost before anyone noticed, precocious kids had learned more about computers and how they work than most of the adults who earned a living with them as typists or reservation clerks.

Individuals responsible for computer security, many of them unskilled in the field, by and large did not anticipate an invasion of hackers and were caught unprepared. The passwords of legitimate clients tended to be single words or names easily discovered with a computerized dictionary *(pages 21-25).* Computer specialists at Bell Laboratories in Murray Hill, New Jersey, once showed that they could guess fully half the passwords in use there. Furthermore, passwords were sometimes handed out carelessly, and they were changed too infrequently to guard against compromise. Computer managers failed to remove passwords—easy-to-guess ones like "demo," "system" and "test"—recorded in the machine by manufacturers to aid initial testing and installation. Discovered early on by hackers, they gave easy access to the most advanced equipment.

The term "hacker" may have originated at M.I.T. as students' jargon for class-mates who labored nights in the computer lab. In the beginning, hackers were Robin Hoods. They stole computer time from the university system, which was rich in this precious commodity, and donated it to "poor" students, who often felt that they needed more than their allocation of processing hours to test programs they had written. But in the early 1980s, hackers and hacking acquired a reputation for reckless maliciousness as a result of widely publicized incidents in which youthful computer enthusiasts infiltrated their way by keyboard and telephone into data banks where they had no business.

• Members of the 414s, a Milwaukee group named after the telephone area code for eastern Wisconsin, were reported to have surreptitiously entered more than 60 computer systems, including ones at Los Alamos National Laboratory in New Mexico, an important United States nuclear-weapons research facility, and Memorial Sloan-Kettering Cancer Center in New York City.

• A Los Angeles high-school student, probing a computer at a state university, gained entry and—"just for the fun of it"—destroyed research data that graduate students had painstakingly assembled and stored in the computer.

• De Paul University in Chicago suffered one computer breakdown after another. Teen-age computer enthusiasts had broken into the system and written a computer program that deleted portions of the operating system, the basic instructions that allow computers to function.

• *Newsweek* reporter Richard Sandza wrote a story about hackers based on messages that he, under the alias Montana Wildhack, had exchanged with them using computer bulletin boards, the electronic equivalent of the cork-and-thumbtack variety. Bulletin boards are maintained by organizations or individuals to enable people to trade information by computer. Sandza's reward: hundreds of harassing telephone calls, death threats, his credit-card numbers traded among hackers across the United States.

THE TOOLS FOR TRESPASSING

The equipment required for such mischief has become no more expensive than a classy skiing outfit or a top-of-the-line bicycle. A few hundred dollars buys a modem and a modest but adequate home computer that can display messages on a television screen. With both the computer and a telephone plugged into the modem, electronic trespassing can be remarkably simple. To begin, all a hacker needs is the number of a telephone line hooked up to a computer somewhere. Such numbers are generally available for the asking from members of computer clubs; the numbers can also be found posted on computer bulletin boards accessible by modem. The same facility might yield a simple program that tries all the telephone numbers in an exchange, recording the ones that answer with the distinctive voice of a computer. The voice might be that of a computer wired into Telenet, Tymnet, Datapack or Europac, special telephone networks set up for computers to communicate over. It could be another bulletin board—or something even more exciting. Breaking into the computer might then require only a few hours of testing likely passwords.

The ease with which hackers gambol among others' computers has gained them considerable notoriety, and deservedly so. Computer hacking, said one college student, "is a game. It is a chance to show you are clever." However, once into a strange computer system, "you need more knowledge than most of these kids possess to do no damage." The 414s purposely deleted the record of their attempts to gain access to Sloan-Kettering's computer in an attempt to erase their tracks. The slight damage they did was easily repaired. But if the group had accidentally deleted patient records, the resulting interruptions of treatment could well have had fatal consequences.

Hackers are often unconcerned with the havoc their computer probing might wreak. As one participant at a hackers' convention near San Francisco put it: "Once the rockets go up, who cares where they come down? That is the hacker ethic, too." Statements from what might be called the radical left among hackers sound even more anarchic. "Philosophically," pronounced Richard Stallman, a self-professed hacker and expert programmer who has placed some of his best work in the public domain, "we don't believe in property rights."

AID FOR THE INSECURE

With computers, data and programs vulnerable not only to hackers but to out-and-out criminals, duplicitous insiders and acts of God, a new industry has sprung up to keep all components safe. There are companies that provide storage for preserving duplicate copies of irreplaceable data, the loss of which has put more than one company out of business. The facilities are as secure against theft as a bank vault—and far superior in the protection they offer against changes in temperature and humidity that can shorten the life of magnetic disks and tapes. New methods are being explored to verify the identity of someone seeking access to a computer and the information it contains. One technique matches the pattern of blood vessels in the retina—as unique as a fingerprint—against a catalogue of individuals' retinal images stored in the computer; similar comparisons are possible using the distinctive tone and timbre of a person's voice or the inimitable outline of a hand *(pages 45-57)*.

Other companies specialize in computers designed to block signals that would otherwise emanate from monitors and keyboards or from deep inside a machine's circuitry and allow an eavesdropper to listen in on the computer's business *(pages 94-97)*. Still other manufacturers produce computers designed to operate flawlessly under extremes of heat, cold and humidity, and even after being run over by a truck. So-called fault-tolerant computers rarely stumble even when something goes awry inside that would bring an ordinary computer to a halt. These computers are much to be desired for such applications as air-traffic control systems, where a sudden shutdown could cause calamity.

Specially designed operating systems—combinations of programs that contain the instructions necessary for a computer to perform fundamental tasks such as retrieving data from storage and moving it around inside the computer—closely monitor the activities of everyone using the system to prevent even those most skilled in manipulating the machine from sneaking a look at any information they are not entitled to see. Confidential messages that must move through communications channels where anyone with the right equipment could intercept them may be encrypted so as to thoroughly garble the contents.

With so many security options to choose from, an army of consultants has arisen. Selling advice about what ought to be protected and the best way to go about doing so, they are most often entrepreneurs who go into business for

Mapping a System's Vulnerabilities

The hardest kind of computer system to protect is one with multiple users, some of whom are connected to the mainframe from remote stations. The typical multi-user system, shown below and on the following two pages, is vulnerable at many points, not unlike a house with numerous doors and windows. The more people and hardware involved, the greater the chance of trouble.

Physical threats to a system represent one broad category of

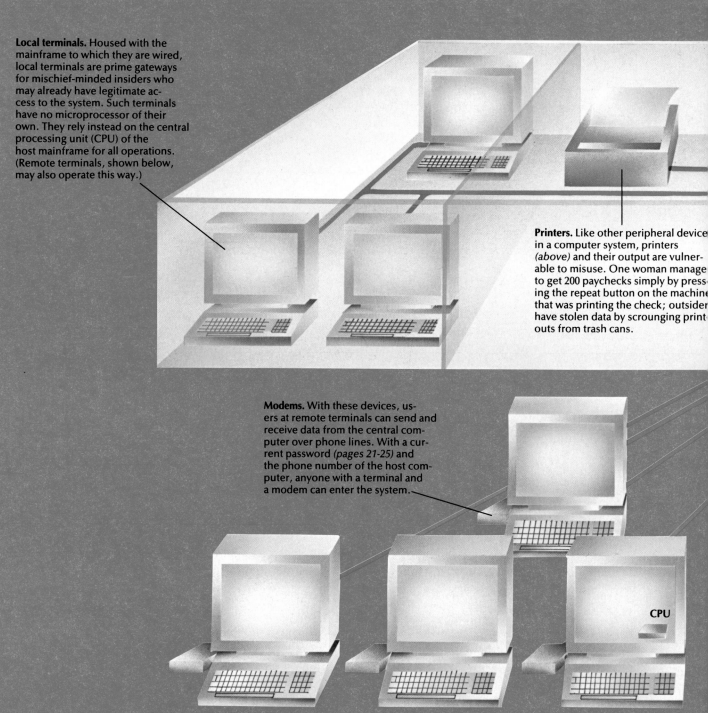

Local terminals. Housed with the mainframe to which they are wired, local terminals are prime gateways for mischief-minded insiders who may already have legitimate access to the system. Such terminals have no microprocessor of their own. They rely instead on the central processing unit (CPU) of the host mainframe for all operations. (Remote terminals, shown below, may also operate this way.)

Printers. Like other peripheral devices in a computer system, printers *(above)* and their output are vulnerable to misuse. One woman managed to get 200 paychecks simply by pressing the repeat button on the machine that was printing the check; outsiders have stolen data by scrounging printouts from trash cans.

Modems. With these devices, users at remote terminals can send and receive data from the central computer over phone lines. With a current password *(pages 21-25)* and the phone number of the host computer, anyone with a terminal and a modem can enter the system.

CPU

risk. Surges in electrical power—caused by lightning, for example—can burn out delicate circuitry. The computer system must be protected against flood or fire as well as against the mundane environmental hazards of heat and high humidity, which are capable of interfering with sensitive electronic operations. But more worrisome by far is the physical threat that is posed by humans.

Simple carelessness is one problem: Dropping and damaging a disk pack can render the data stored on it inaccessible; spilling liquid into a keyboard or disk drive can disable its electronics. Sabotage, too, is a possibility. Inside users can take advantage of their ready access to vandalize equipment; outsiders can cut cables or plant bombs. In most cases, however, the aim of those who attempt to breach a computer system's security is not to damage the system itself but to tamper with or steal the information it contains.

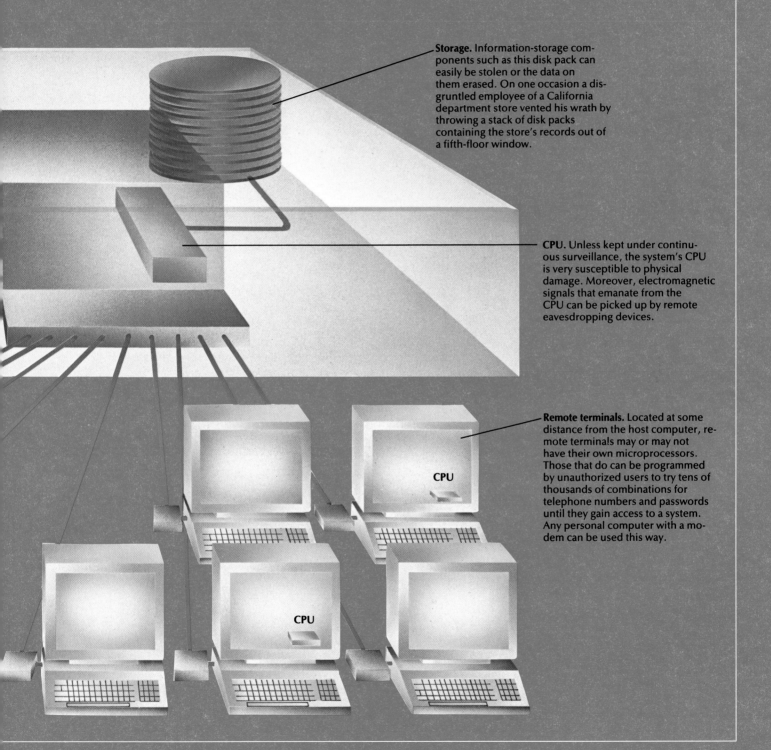

Storage. Information-storage components such as this disk pack can easily be stolen or the data on them erased. On one occasion a disgruntled employee of a California department store vented his wrath by throwing a stack of disk packs containing the store's records out of a fifth-floor window.

CPU. Unless kept under continuous surveillance, the system's CPU is very susceptible to physical damage. Moreover, electromagnetic signals that emanate from the CPU can be picked up by remote eavesdropping devices.

Remote terminals. Located at some distance from the host computer, remote terminals may or may not have their own microprocessors. Those that do can be programmed by unauthorized users to try tens of thousands of combinations for telephone numbers and passwords until they gain access to a system. Any personal computer with a modem can be used this way.

CPU

CPU

The Trespasser's Devious Methods

Once a computer system has been penetrated, the intruder can use the system's own software to pilfer information (and often money as well) and to erase or create data. Such software includes operating systems, the programs that serve to coordinate a computer's internal housekeeping functions; utility programs, which perform tasks such as copying data from one storage medium to another; and application programs, which allow users to do specific jobs such as bookkeeping or word processing.

When not in use, both software and data reside in external storage on disks or tape. To start up a system or get access to a program or data file, a user must bring software and data into the computer's temporary memory—also called random-access memory, or RAM. (Information in RAM disappears when the machine is turned off; so-called read-only memory, or ROM, holds permanent instructions for the machine.)

An intruder intent on tampering with a system's programs and data can do so while this information is en route to or from temporary memory or storage. More often, however, the tampering is done before the information is put into the system. In a practice called data diddling, for instance, students' grades might be altered before they are entered into a school's computerized records.

More difficult to achieve—and to detect—is an invasion known as a trap door. Usually, this involves a programmer's writing into an otherwise secure program a secret sequence of instructions. The program is then put into the system, where it operates normally—but the programmer can invoke the hidden instructions with a special code to gain unauthorized access to restricted parts of the system. A similar ploy, equally difficult to trace, is the time bomb, an instruction that triggers computer action, such as the payment of money or the deletion of incriminating records, at a fixed future date when the perpetrator is far away.

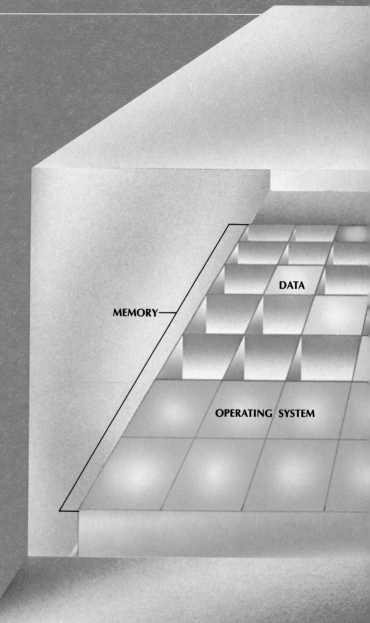

MEMORY

DATA

OPERATING SYSTEM

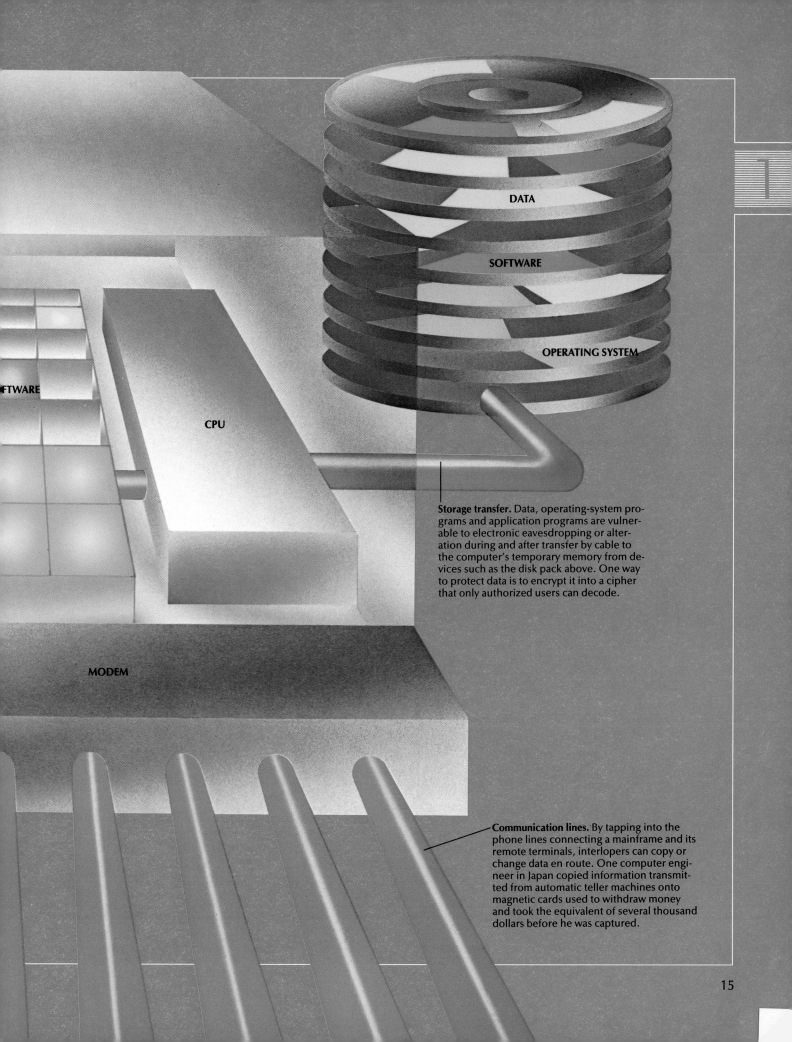

DATA

SOFTWARE

OPERATING SYSTEM

FTWARE

CPU

MODEM

Storage transfer. Data, operating-system programs and application programs are vulnerable to electronic eavesdropping or alteration during and after transfer by cable to the computer's temporary memory from devices such as the disk pack above. One way to protect data is to encrypt it into a cipher that only authorized users can decode.

Communication lines. By tapping into the phone lines connecting a mainframe and its remote terminals, interlopers can copy or change data en route. One computer engineer in Japan copied information transmitted from automatic teller machines onto magnetic cards used to withdraw money and took the equivalent of several thousand dollars before he was captured.

themselves after serving in a similar capacity with a large company, the government or the armed forces. Others have come to the profession with years of firsthand experience working the other side of the fence.

Consider John Maxfield. As a child growing up in Michigan in the mid-1950s, Maxfield was intrigued by electronics. At the age of 12, he built a primitive computer. Then, in his teens, he became a "phone phreak," the name given to people who manipulated the telephone system by electronic trickery. Phone phreaks might be considered the original hackers, and John Maxfield was one of the best. Independently of others, he invented both the so-called black box and a successor, the blue box, to avoid paying for long-distance telephone calls.

Wired to the telephone, the black box reduced the voltage used to send a voice over a telephone to a level that was too low to trip the voice-activated switch at the telephone company that controlled billing, but still high enough for the voice to be heard. The blue box had keys that reproduced single-frequency tones available to telephone operators but not to callers from ordinary telephones, which produce double-frequency tones. After dialing a number, pressing the proper sequence of keys before the telephone was answered interrupted the call but kept the line open. Thereafter, any call the phone phreak dialed was seen as originating, not from his own number, but from the number at the other end of the open line, to which the call was billed.

TURNCOAT HACKERS

Maxfield struck a deal with the telephone company: To escape prosecution, he agreed never to reveal the secrets he had discovered. He went on to a modest life in Detroit, installing office telephone systems and repairing teletypewriter equipment. In his spare time he toyed with computers, in 1979 becoming the sysop, or system operator, of the Southwest Michigan Computer Club's electronic bulletin board, one of the first in the United States.

Over the years, Maxfield had reformed to the degree that he was offended by acts of software piracy committed with the aid of the bulletin board. It was not unusual to see copyrighted computer games—which, to the bulletin board, are merely long and complicated messages—illegally posted there, free for the taking by any club member. After learning of an FBI inquiry into the theft of such games, he offered his services in running to ground not only game pirates but phone phreaks and anyone else he could discover illegally touring the nation's computer systems. The government eagerly accepted.

"In a way," he said later, "it was the ultimate hacker challenge, to hack the hackers." Granted federal authority to phreak, Maxfield became known on hacker bulletin boards as Cable Pair, an accommodating fellow, eager to explain to those he took into his confidence everything he knew about computers and phreaking. Whenever he learned the identity of a lawless correspondent, he would turn the facts over to the FBI for action. "I've lost track of the number of people," he said. "I count as one of my 'kills' anyone I've provided information on who was subsequently arrested."

Cable Pair operated for 18 months or so before he unintentionally compromised his own identity: He took his evidence directly to a business victimized by hackers instead of going through his FBI contact, and word of his true role soon leaked to the hacker underworld. His cover blown, Maxfield became the target of other hackers bent on getting even. The harassment compelled him to change his telephone number several times, a practice that severely disrupted his teletypewriter repair business. So he switched careers and founded Board Scan to keep tabs on hacker bulletin boards, reporting to credit-card and telephone companies any customer account numbers that he found there. "It was dirty business," Maxfield recalled of his days as Cable Pair, "but I don't think the hackers can be allowed to continue, because if they do, they will ultimately bring us all down."

MORE BARK THAN BITE

Security consultant Robert Courtney, formerly of IBM, has asserted that, for all the furor surrounding hackers, they "have done less damage to corporate computer systems than overflowing lavatories." Moreover, they have not even come close to breaching the security of computers, such as the ones at the North American Aerospace Defense Command (NORAD), that manage the defenses of the United States. Nor are they likely to: Such computers are linked to no public network that might let a hacker enter. Robert Morris, a computer-security expert at Bell Laboratories, has often been a member of "Tiger Teams" that test the vulnerability of computers by trying to outsmart their defenses. He says, "I do not know any way even remotely possible of getting into those computers without a breach of trust."

The security of other computer networks, some of which may carry confidential research data, can be improved by the addition of such devices as dial-back machines. After confirming the identity of the person seeking access by modem, a dial-back box hangs up. It then dials the number authorized for that person to verify that a stranger is not trying to hack into the system from a different location. Not every computer is worthy of such measures. For example, the Los Alamos computer that the 414s broke into contained no secrets; it was being used mainly to experiment with computer mail systems.

Genuine criminals intent on theft or destruction are no more difficult than hackers to keep at bay. Donn Parker of SRI International, a scientific research organization interested in the illegal use of computers, once remarked that only rarely do "we get a crime in which somebody has done something intelligent, and it makes our day." Most of the cases that come to light are, in his view, disappointingly unsophisticated and depend primarily on the kind of simple laxity that hackers exploit.

In 1978, a man named Stanley Rifkin stole $10.2 million dollars from a Los Angeles bank simply by posing as a consultant hired to improve the operation of the bank's communications center, where computer messages for transferring funds originate. By interviewing console operators there, he collected all the computer passwords and bank codes necessary to pose as an officer of the institution over the phone and have the funds transferred to a New York bank account and thence to Switzerland. He was apprehended—and sentenced to eight years in prison—only because he bragged about the caper to his lawyer, trusting that his attorney would not report the crime because of the confidential relationship between attorney and client. Unable to tolerate such an abuse, the lawyer turned his client in to the FBI.

Bell Labs expert Morris was once asked to help a company protect its data. After an interview with an officer of the firm, Morris happened past a room labeled Message Center. "I walked around the room unescorted, with no badge or identification," he recalled. "I looked at each terminal. I spent ten or fifteen minutes there and no one asked me who I was." That was ample time to learn all he needed to break into the organization's computers.

Gaps in security like the one Morris walked through can be plugged simply by keeping a door locked; Stanley Rifkin would have been thwarted had anyone asked him for identification. It is more difficult to prevent crimes by those who have the key to the lock or who have valid identification. They need not break into the system; they are already inside. And there they might become so-called data diddlers, altering the information held by the computer. For example, according to a British science periodical, most of the computer crimes reported in Great Britain involve false information put into a computer: "These frauds are the same in essence as any other kind of embezzlement. They take advantage of gaps in an accounting system and depend on the criminal knowing he will not be quickly discovered."

In 1980, such a crime took place in Baltimore. A Social Security clerk, Janet Braintree Blair, observed that new applicants sometimes were paid a smaller lump sum than they were entitled to when they began to collect benefits. Unlike the recipients, Blair understood precisely how the lump sum was calculated. When she came upon one that was incorrect, she requested a check from the computer for the additional funds, replacing the rightful payee's name and address with her own. The next morning, she restored the original address. Blair mailed herself no less than $108,000 in fraudulent Social Security checks before being caught and convicted for her embezzlement.

LARCENY AT THE TOP

High officials of an organization can use computers to defraud the public on a scale never before possible, as was revealed in 1973 with the Equity Funding Corporation, which passed itself off as a multimillion-dollar insurance and financial conglomerate. In that instance, the president of the company and several of his underlings issued 64,000 bogus insurance policies. Taken together, the policies that an insurance company issues present a distinctive profile based on such factors as amounts of coverage, size of premiums, and numbers of policies canceled and benefits paid. By using the computer to make certain that, as a group, the false policies were indistinguishable in these and other important characteristics from the company's legitimate policies, the perpetrators of the fraud concealed it for 10 years. When the ruse eventually was exposed, Equity Funding went under, leaving 7,000 investors holding worthless stock and more than 50 lawsuits to be settled in the wake of the disaster.

For the Equity Funding fraud to succeed for as long as it did required the collusion of a handful of computer programmers in the actuarial department, where insurance risks are calculated. They were the ones who made certain that the bogus policies mimicked the real ones closely enough to avert detection. Programmers like these, who have been granted access to the very heart of the computer, present the greatest danger. With their savvy, they can subvert computer systems in ways that may never be detected.

Among their weapons are Trojan horses, logic bombs and viruses. A Trojan horse is a program that, like the gift that doomed ancient Troy, conceals agents of ruin; they operate invisibly whenever the program is invoked, stealing data, passwords or worse. An expert programmer can write a Trojan horse that is invisible to any but the most detailed investigation. Logic bombs are set to go off at a future time or event. For example, a programmer might write a logic bomb to wreak revenge if the programmer were ever dismissed. A program of a few lines, secreted away among the tens of thousands of instructions that constitute a computer operating system, could command the computer to remove every employee from the payroll if one particular name were ever deleted. Viruses, as the name suggests, are infectious, data-gobbling programs that spread like plague between computers connected to one another through networks *(Chapter 3)*.

Some experts play down the threat posed by computer programmers. "Contrary to all the publicity," Robert Courtney has asserted, "we really do not have a technical security problem." By his count, only seven of a thousand computer break-ins reported over a recent four-year period were the work of professional programmers. "In five of the seven cases, the programmers stole money just by using the system as it was designed to be used, while in the other two, programmers carried out robberies by modifying existing programs illegally."

ASSESSING THE DAMAGE
The multitude of chinks in computer armor add up to substantial potential for harm worldwide, whoever the perpetrators might be. A South American bank reportedly lost $13 million in a fraud that was not discovered until six months after the event. In Milan, Italy, several bank employees transferred large sums from customers' computerized accounts to their own. In a single year, Japan reported 472 fraudulent transactions involving automatic teller machines.

Some computer-security authorities do not believe that an undiscovered swamp of computer crime lies in wait. Others, with comparable credentials, contend that unreported crimes far outnumber those that come to light. They point out that clever crimes may never be discovered. And should they be, the victims—especially banks and large corporations—may decline to prosecute. According to Robert Courtney, "Shareholders, voters and policyholders all look on major fraud as evidence of gross mismanagement, and usually they are right. If a company decides to prosecute, the crime gets into the newspapers. This means that the bigger the crime, the lower the probability that it will be prosecuted." Following this line of reasoning, estimates of the monetary damages vary so widely that they qualify as little more than wild guesses. In England, *The Daily Telegraph* calculated that computer-related frauds cost British industry "between 500 million and 2.5 billion pounds a year." In the United States, the figure ranges from $300 million to $5 billion.

A victim who files charges against a criminal will discover that breaking into a computer electronically is not the same as robbing a bank at gunpoint. In the absence of laws specifically protecting computer data from theft or misdirection by computer, such intrusions and thefts might not even be illegal. Moreover, a crime might begin at a computer in one state, ravage a computer in another, and spirit the booty to yet another state or even to a foreign country. Questions arise: Where was the crime committed? Who has jurisdiction in prosecuting it?

Some jurists have called for federal legislation. John C. Armor, a Baltimore attorney, has pointed out that computer criminals have exploited the same kind of gap in the law that permitted Jesse James so much success as a bank robber in the Old West. In Armor's view, "James was the first bank robber to make a science of his profession." Recognizing that his activities were illegal only under state laws, James began to choose banks close to a state line; once he made it across the border, his chances of being caught—and brought to trial—decreased dramatically. The government's somewhat belated response was to make robbery of federally chartered banks a federal crime.

Similar laws against computer crime may well be worth having on the books, locally as well as nationally. Many states, as well as the federal government, have taken action since 1978, when Arizona enacted the first computer-crime laws. But legislation alone will no more likely end computer crime than laws against breaking and entering have stopped burglary. City dwellers and suburbanites bolt doors and windows to protect their possessions; managers of computer systems must take similar measures to keep out thieves, vandals and curious kids.

THE PRICE OF COMPUTER SECURITY

The cost of denying such miscreants entry to computer systems is one reason why, with few exceptions outside the military and the national defense industry, computer security has received all too little attention. There is the price that one might expect to pay for the tools of security: equipment ranging from locks on doors to computerized gate-keepers that stand watch against hackers, special software that prevents employees from peeking at data that is none of their concern *(pages 73-85)*, a staff trained to be alert for people seeking unauthorized access. The bill can range from hundreds of dollars to many thousands, depending on the degree of assurance sought.

But there is also a hidden price, one paid in time and inconvenience. Often, new work rules must be imposed, disrupting the old way of doing things. No longer can identifying passwords be easy-to-remember birthdates and nick-names, nor can their less-memorable replacements be posted at the computer for ready reference. The process of encoding and decoding data slows the computer, as well as the progress of workers who may already be saddled with impossible deadlines. Clip-on badges, which wrinkle blouses and shirts, may be found necessary to control access to a computer room. Such complications inhibit the adoption of effective computer-security measures.

It may even be necessary to make the computer less "friendly," in the vernacular of data processing. If gaining access to a computer is easy for those authorized to do so, the process may offer few obstacles to a determined outsider trying to get in. A computer system that teaches insiders how to use it, for example, can offer the same assistance to unauthorized people.

Managers of computer systems can find it perplexing to decide what information ought to be protected and to what length they should pursue the matter. No combination of technologies promises unbreachable security. Experts in the field agree that someone with sufficient resources can crack almost any computer defense. And the attack need not be direct. For example, it may cost a criminal far less in time and money to bribe a disloyal employee for the key that deciphers a company's encrypted messages than to assemble the computer power needed to crack the code. In the end, everyone who works with computers bears a measure of responsibility for their security, whether it is to decide what measures should be taken, to maintain those safeguards or simply not to betray them.

20

Turning Away an Attack with a Word

Passwords are a multi-user computer system's usual first line of defense against intrusion. A password may be any combination of alphabetic and numeric characters, to a maximum length set by the particular system. Most systems can accommodate passwords up to 40 characters long; some can handle as many as 80 characters. Would-be users are not allowed into the system until they confirm their identity and access rights by keying in the password that matches the one on file with their name.

Since even legitimate users may make typing mistakes, many systems allow a minute for three to five tries before refusing access or breaking the telephone connection. Unless the system has security methods sophisticated enough to detect repeated entry attempts from the same terminal, an unauthorized person is free to try again at will. Outside hackers who have found (or guessed) at least the name of a legitimate user can thus program their own computers not only to dial the target system repeatedly but, in an approach known as a brute-force attack, to keep trying different combinations of characters in hopes of hitting upon a password that works.

Ideally, then, a password should be constructed so as to withstand a brute-force attack long enough to make it not worth the hacker's time. To this end, multi-user systems often have a security officer who assigns every user a password randomly generated by computer. For each individual character, the computer chooses from among 36 possibilities (the 26 letters of the alphabet plus the 10 decimal numbers). The longer the password, the more possibilities a hacker's password-guessing program must work through.

The catch is that a long, randomly generated password can also be very difficult to remember, tempting a user to write it down, which immediately makes it a security risk. But passwords that are easy to remember—a mother's first name, say, or a significant word—are susceptible to discovery for other reasons, chief among them that they are gathered into handy sources such as dictionaries. With a dictionary of 2,000 common names, for instance, a hacker could find a first name, even a long one, in an average of five hours of repeated tries.

On the following pages, a metaphorical computer-as-fortress is used to illustrate the relative security of random and meaningful passwords. The best compromise, of course, is a password that is as difficult to discover as a random assortment, but has a nonrandom meaning known only to its owner.

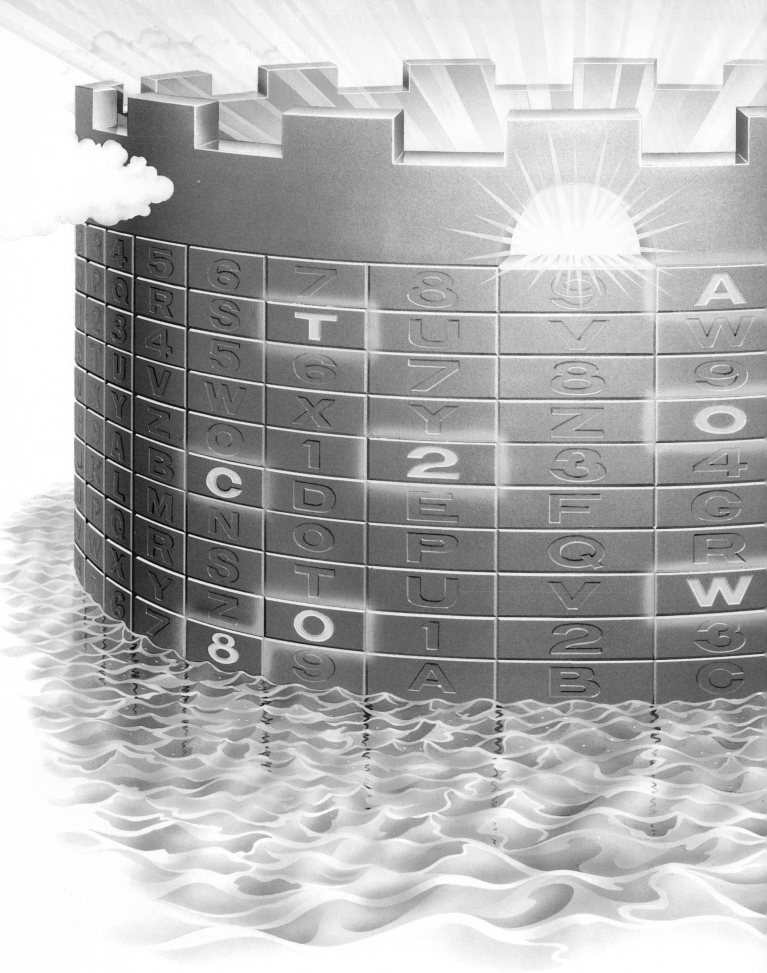

The Pros and Cons of Randomness

In this analogy of a computer system as a fortress, the password is composed of 10 characters—ATA02CTW08—each selected from 36 alphanumeric possibilities at each of the fort's 10 tiers. An attacker would have to find the correct combination to align the characters vertically and unlock the drawbridge. Even a computer that enabled the attacker to test one million guesses per second—a power far in excess of the personal-computer systems typically available to hackers—would require, on average, close to 60 years to ferret out a random 10-character password from the 3,700,000,000,000,000 possible combinations.

Random passwords. As the chart below demonstrates, increasing the length of a random password can make it drastically more difficult to discover. With each additional character, both the number of possible combinations and the average time required to find the password increase exponentially. However, passwords made up of truly random combinations are harder to remember the longer they get.

Number of Characters	Possible Combinations	Average Time to Discover
1	36	6 minutes
2	1,300	4 hours
3	47,000	5 days
4	1,700,000	6 months
5	60,000,000	19 years
6	2,000,000,000	630 years
7	78,000,000,000	25,000 years
8	2,800,000,000,000	890,000 years
9	100,000,000,000,000	32,000,000 years
10	3,700,000,000,000,000	1,200,000,000 years

The Varying Security of Memorable Words

The alternative to a randomly generated password is one chosen because it is easy to remember—a set of initials, for instance, or the name of a favorite aunt. The key to the security of such a mnemonic device is not its length per se but whether it can be found in a relatively small, ready-made source such as a name dictionary. The password for the fortress shown here is the same length—10 characters—as the password on page 22, but this one is the word "instrument." A hacker using word-processor software designed to check the spelling of 60,000 words can find a word from that list in an average of only seven days.

The best mnemonic devices combine the advantage of easy recall with the security of randomness. A familiar phrase or line of poetry, for instance, can be compressed to form a combination of letters that would never appear in a dictionary. Similarly, the password on page 22 looks like a meaningless jumble, but in fact it is composed of the initials and birth months of the user's two grandmothers—a combination particularly easy for the user to remember.

Mnemonic passwords. As shown below, so long as the mnemonic password is not a common name or a real word, security increases with length. The greater the number of possibilities a hacker must sort through, the better the chances of a password's remaining undiscovered.

How Chosen	Example	Number of Possibilities	Average Time to Discover
Name (short/long)	Al/Charlotte	2,000 (name dictionary)	5 hours
Word (short/long)	a/photoduplication	60,000 (spelling checker)	7 days
Two words together	dogcat	3,600,000,000	1,140 years
Mix of initials and significant dates	ATA02CTW08	3,700,000,000,000,000	1,200,000,000 years
First line of a poem	Maryhadalittlelamb	10,000,000,000,000,000,000,000,000,000	3,000,000,000,000,000,000,000 years
First two letters of each word of a poem's first line	Mahaalila	100,000,000,000,000	32,000,000 years

Warding Off Physical Perils

Perpetrators of computer-related crimes, like other kinds of criminals, often seek a degree of anonymity after they have been found out, even though their cases are a matter of public record. So it is with a former computer-operations supervisor for Imperial Chemical Industries (ICI) who, preferring to keep his name to himself, goes by the pseudonym Jon. As Jon recounted his story some time later, his caper began innocently enough. Eager to tighten computer security at Imperial Chemical's installations in the Netherlands, he was reading a book on the subject when he came across an account of valuable computer tapes that had been stolen and held for ransom.

Jon was intrigued by this crime; he, too, had access to tapes and disks, ones that contained key records of the London-based multinational's extensive European operations. He discussed the case with a colleague, a computer-systems analyst at Imperial, and during idle moments, the two men fantasized about pulling off a "kidnapping" like the one described in the book.

Soon thereafter, when Jon was passed over for promotion, greed and disgruntlement brought the fantasy to life. On a quiet Saturday in 1977, he drove his car to two different company installations and simply signed out the data tapes and disks, as he was authorized to do. He and his systems-analyst colleague, whom he had enlisted as an accomplice, now had in their possession 48 sets of disks and 54 tapes—the originals plus the backup, or duplicate, copies, which had been stored at the second site. The two thieves stashed the purloined files in a rented garage.

For the return of the data to ICI, the men demanded a ransom of £275,000—nearly $500,000—to be delivered in London. This appraisal of the stolen data's value was a conservative one; the files contained vital information such as payroll records and pension-fund investments, as well as accounts payable and receivable. Officials of Imperial Chemical estimated that if the missing data could not be recovered, the company would have to spend two million pounds to reconstruct the information and would lose a like amount in revenues. To demonstrate to ICI what would happen to the hostage data if the company did not comply promptly with the ransom demand, the two thieves sent along a partially erased backup tape.

Imperial Chemical Industries capitulated. At the appointed hour, an ICI representative appeared at the rendezvous in Piccadilly Circus, the center of London's hustle and bustle, carrying a black briefcase stuffed with ransom money in £5 and £10 notes. As instructed, he stood on the curb and, feeling rather foolish, held out the briefcase at arm's length. The two extortionists roared up on a motorcycle and lurched to a stop. As one of them reached for the loot, they received instead a rude greeting. ICI had tipped off Scotland Yard, and 10 London bobbies, disguised as street sweepers, collared the none-too-clever kidnappers and packed them off to jail.

The affair had a happy ending for ICI, which got its precious data back from

From bolts of lightning to seemingly inconsequential specks of dust, physical hazards to computers abound. Prudent measures should be taken against the most threatening, but the best insurance is to store duplicate copies of data—and even a spare computer—in a safe place in case of disaster.

27

conductive filaments serve to dissipate static electricity before it can build to a spark. The other solution resides in the computer itself; most modern machines are built to shrug off the average jolt of static electricity by routing it safely past sensitive components.

For the most part, the climate inside a computer facility is under the control of the men and women who manage that facility. But the electrical power that sustains computers can, at times, be so capricious that it may appear to be out of control altogether. Unpredictable fluctuations in the normal power supply often cause trouble that has nothing to do with wayward lizards. These surges and sags,

Tamper-Resistant Cards to Fight Forgery and Fraud

Locks and keys are a traditional way to limit access to secure areas. But keys have a way of getting stolen or copied. The people concerned with the security of computer systems have thus looked for ways to render keylike devices ineffective if they fall into the wrong hands.

Three types of card-keys designed to foil fraudulent use are illustrated here. Each of these card-keys can employ an identifying number or password that is encoded in the card itself, and all are produced by techniques beyond the reach of the average computer criminal. One card makes use of a patented manufacturing process called watermark magnetics, which was inspired by the watermarks on paper currency. A 12-digit number built into the card's magnetic strip during manufacture cannot be counterfeited.

The other two cards have the capability of storing thousands of times more data than the roughly 2,000 bits contained in a magnetic strip. In optical memory cards (OMCs), data is encoded in one of two ways: by a photolithographic process during manufacture (in which case it is impossible for the card's owner to alter the information) or by a special low-powered laser device purchased by the user. In either case, the data takes the form of coded pits in the surface of the card, which is read by an optical scanner.

Smart cards contain a microchip that is, in effect, a small computer with enough memory to hold both programs and data. The read-only memory holds the card's operating system, and the random-access memory holds temporary results of computations (it does not retain information when the card is disconnected from a power source). In addition, the chip contains a programmable read-only memory that may be altered only under special conditions.

A magnetic watermark. During manufacture of the tape, magnetic particles used to encode the card's permanent identification number are set in zones of varying width at alternating 45-degree angles to the tape's longitudinal axis. Data may then be encoded on the tape, but the identifying structure of the tape itself cannot be altered or copied. A card reader with a special head and circuitry is needed to scan the watermark. _____

Optical memory card (OMC). Minute dots representing binary zeros and ones are either photographically etched onto the storage strip during manufacture or burned in later with a tiny, low-powered laser beam. The card, which can hold the equivalent of a 400-page book in its 3¼-by-½-inch strip, is sealed with a protective layer that cannot be removed without destroying the data and invalidating the card. _____

Smart card. The card's penny-size microchip contains a processor and three types of memory, totaling 21,800 bits, for storing programs and data. Sensitive information, such as the cardholder's password, is kept in the so-called secret zone of the card's programmable read-only memory; this zone is encoded during manufacture and is not accessible even to the card's owner. _____

known as transients, sometimes trigger logic errors that cause programs to go awry or data stored within a computer to be changed inadvertently. In extreme instances, a surge can burn out computer circuitry.

If the power stumbles for as little as $1/100$ of a second, data stored in the machine's temporary memory can be lost. A longer power loss may cause a disk drive's record-and-playback heads, which transfer information from computer to disk and back, to crash on the disk's fragile magnetic surface. Under normal conditions, a record-and-playback head never touches the surface of the disk. Instead, it floats about $1/100$ of an inch above the disk, supported on a current of air

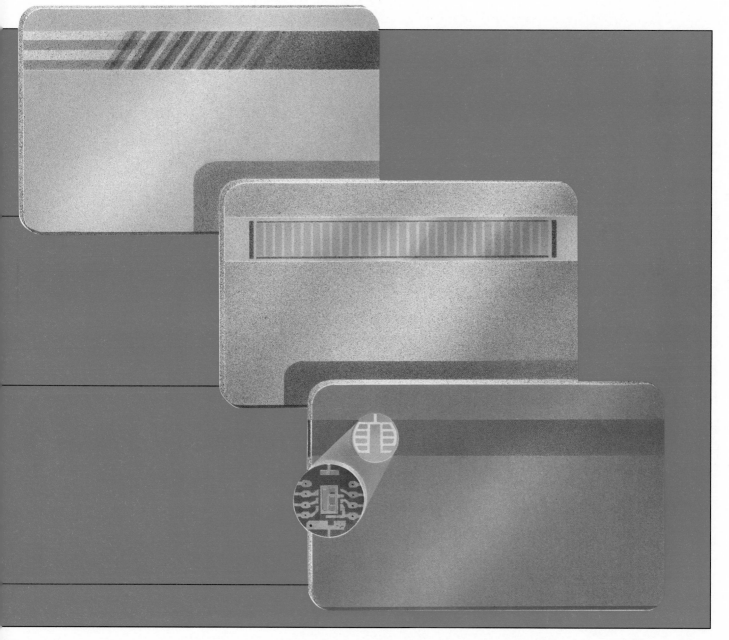

created by the disk's spinning below the head at high speed. A head crash, as it is known in the trade, gouges the disk and eradicates data recorded there. To prevent this catastrophe, some disk drives are made so that they will retract their heads at the first flicker in the power supply.

Transients occur routinely when electrical equipment stops or starts anywhere along the power line. As a rule, though, only machinery that consumes large amounts of electricity will produce noticeable effects. For example, when an air-conditioner compressor cycles off or an elevator comes to a stop to discharge or take on passengers, the sharp change in voltage can affect the power supply to nearby computers.

On rare occasions, a conglomeration of small devices can cause similar difficulties. Problems with a computer system in Southend, England, were traced to voltage surges occurring precisely at 10:30 p.m., the end of the television broadcast day and the time when many residents of the city switched off their television sets almost in unison.

During a violent thunderstorm, lightning that surges through power lines can fry a computer's innards or perform other evil deeds. At a computer center in Los Angeles during one such storm, lightning missed the machines but somehow passed through the metal shelving in the data library, generating a magnetic field of such strength that it erased information worth millions of dollars from tapes archived there.

DEFENDING AGAINST TRANSIENTS

Protection from the sometimes disastrous effects of electrical surges and sags is available through a variety of devices. For small machines, some of which consume no more power than a 250-watt light bulb, a surge suppressor or voltage regulator is adequate defense against power transients and costs little. Surge suppressors function by diverting sudden power increases before they peak. Voltage regulators for computers perform the same service and, in addition, fill in voltage dips before they become deep enough to affect the computer. But these devices have too little capacity to work for most large computers, which, together with disk drives and other equipment, burn power at many times the rate of desktop models. Such a system is commonly protected by a motor-generator set, which effectively isolates the computer from brief, random ups and downs in the power supply. To do so, an electric motor uses electricity from the power company to run a generator, which in turn creates new, smoothly flowing electricity for the computer.

However, surge suppressors, voltage regulators and motor-generator sets cannot save a computer from a total power failure, even one that lasts for only a fraction of a second. Salvation in that event is offered by a so-called UPS, or uninterruptible power supply. A UPS system is made up of a complex of electrical apparatus that is built around storage batteries; it not only filters out transients but provides instantaneous backup power during a blackout. The batteries do run down, of course, but they can sustain computers long enough either to shut down the system in an orderly fashion (without loss of data) or to crank up an auxiliary power supply.

Auxiliary power can be expensive. Multiple diesel generators and a roomful of switching equipment to connect them to the computers can raise the cost of backing up a large UPS system, consisting of hundreds of storage batteries, to as much as one million dollars. At the other end of the spectrum, UPS systems for personal computers can be purchased for as little as a few hundred dollars. But there is no comparably economical backup generator. Small gasoline-powered generators, which some homeowners use to run appliances during power failures, are not up to the job.

The shortcomings of such systems were demonstrated by Erik Sandberg-Diment, computer columnist for *The New York Times,* when he plugged a small computer into a 1,200-watt home generator during the blackout imposed on parts of the United States' East Coast by Hurricane Gloria in the autumn of 1985. "Although 1,200 watts is more than enough power to run a personal computer," he wrote afterward, "the quality of current produced by such a putt-putt is simply not refined enough to suit microelectronics. As an experiment, I powered up an old Commodore 64, which promptly acted as if it had lost its mind, its video display turning into snow after a few seconds."

TRIAL BY CONFLAGRATION
As inconvenient and disruptive as power-supply problems may be, they are simple—if sometimes expensive—to solve. But fire, which can flare up outside a computer facility and spread to engulf it, has so many causes and sources that anticipating and defending against all of them is an impractical goal. And when fire rampages through a computer center, it can make the damage caused by a power failure seem trifling.

At a computer center inside the Pentagon, the U.S. military's sprawling headquarters near Washington, D.C., a 300-watt light bulb once was left burning inside a vault where computer tapes were stored. After a time, the bulb had generated so much heat that the ceiling began to smolder. When the door was opened, air rushing into the room brought the fire to life. Before the flames could be extinguished, they had spread to consume three computer systems worth a total of $6.3 million.

Fire is invariably near the top of any risk analysis. Whether accidental or set by arsonists, fires do more damage to computers than almost any other environmental hazard. For example, a study of computer disasters in the United Kingdom confirmed that fire—and its cousin, explosion—accounted for nearly half of the cases surveyed. Moreover, fire is likely to exact a big toll, as the Pentagon's experience illustrates.

Heat is but one component of the threat. Particles of smoke and soot attack the magnetic surfaces of tapes and disks and may continue to work further mischief well after the crisis has passed. In Washington State, volcanic ash from Mount St. Helens' explosive eruption in 1980 ground away data from disk surfaces and ruined delicate disk-drive mechanisms.

Water used to fight a fire can do as much harm as the flames. Water is poison to a computer that is running. Even a small amount of the liquid may cause short circuits that make a computer go haywire, shut it down completely or ruin it permanently. In 1980, an automatic sprinkler system installed at the U.S. Bureau of the Census malfunctioned and turned itself on in the absence of flames or smoke. A fine spray drenched the bureau's computers, and 19 days went by before the machines could be returned to full operation. As a way of protecting equipment from this kind of accident, some computer centers mount large rolls of plastic sheeting on the walls near the computers, so that the plastic can be pulled out at the first drop of water.

Carbon dioxide gas effectively starves a fire of oxygen, forms no corrosive compounds and leaves no residue to clean up. Yet it is rarely used to extinguish major fires involving computer systems; in concentrations high enough to suppress a fire, it can also suffocate humans. In one alarming incident involving this gas, an automatic carbon dioxide fire-fighting system located under the raised floor of a computer installation, where most of the facility's cables were concealed, discharged accidentally one day. Computer personnel evacuated the room without incident, but the dense gas settled into the rooms on the floor below, nearly suffocating several people at work there.

A product called Halon has often been enlisted as the first line of defense in fire control for computer systems. In concentrations of less than 10 percent, this expensive, specially formulated gas effectively smothers flames yet poses no danger of asphyxiation. In a typical application, smoke and heat detectors automatically trigger the release of Halon to suppress any flames that might be present. But Halon is not a coolant, so it must be used in tandem with a sprinkler system. If enough heat is generated by the fire before the Halon puts it out, the sprinklers may go off after all, with resulting water damage.

BRACING FOR THE INEVITABLE
It is axiomatic that diligence in the pursuit of security offers no guarantees. For that reason, government agencies and companies that depend on computers find it prudent to develop and thoroughly test a so-called disaster-recovery plan (DRP). Without one, bouncing back from an emergency may be impossible. In essence, such a plan provides for quick replacement of ruined computers with functioning ones and for equally fast restoration of programs, data and the telephone communications links upon which a system depends. As illustrated by the case of a bank in Minnesota, a disaster-recovery plan can go a long way toward helping a company weather a catastrophe. On Thanksgiving Day, 1982, a fire virtually destroyed Minneapolis' Norwest Bank, causing an estimated $75 million in damage to three major divisions of the bank—pension and profit sharing, data processing and international operations. But all three divisions were back in business at other locations in just two days.

A key element in Norwest's successful recovery—and the cornerstone of all good DRPs—was a provision for storing backup copies of computer programs and data at a secure location well away from the organization's computer center. Hundreds of companies specializing in computer security rent storage for safeguarding backup tapes and disks. For maximum protection against break-ins, bombs or natural disasters, many such installations are built underground or into mountainsides. One fills a space, formerly occupied by a subway-maintenance facility, that extends 100 feet and spans two city blocks below the World Trade Center in New York City.

A typical backup facility stores its customers' computer information and software in a nondescript building where temperature and humidity are rigidly controlled. Multiple alarm systems, guards and surveillance by closed-circuit television ensure that no one can sneak into the building to steal or vandalize the materials deposited there. To protect data and software in transit, operators of some storage sites even provide 24-hour pickup and delivery service in armored, climate-controlled vans.

A few companies go a step further by establishing sites that make it possible for an organization with no fallback computers of its own to resume operations almost before the dust of a disaster has settled. These places come in two forms, known as cold sites and hot sites. A cold site is a room that has been fully outfitted with computer necessities—communications gear, air conditioning and power—but no computers. They are installed after a disaster. A hot site has backup computers and allied equipment plugged in and ready to go. Membership in a hot site can cost $6,000 a month—as much as six times the tariff for a cold site. The higher fee may seem reasonable to businesses such as banks and to government agencies that can ill afford even a day's suspension of operations.

THE HUMAN ELEMENT

A disaster-recovery plan, complete with provisions for off-premises storage and backup processing sites, may also be needed if a company is to withstand the extraordinary variety of outrages that humans have committed against computer systems. People have set them aflame with Molotov cocktails; bombed them with plastique, the terrorist's general-purpose explosive; stabbed them with screwdrivers; and short-circuited them with ordinary keys. One computer was severely beaten by a woman with the spiked heel of her shoe.

As if this arsenal were not enough, rumors and unverified reports of other anticomputer weapons often make the rounds. During the late 1960s, for example, widely circulated stories focused on the purported danger of hand-held magnets. A disgruntled employee armed with a small magnet was said to have erased data from thousands of magnetic tapes in a single night. As it turned out, experiments by the U.S. National Bureau of Standards proved that small magnets were in fact poor weapons indeed for use against electronic data. To erase magnetization of particles of iron oxide on a tape, the magnet must be held no more than a fraction of an inch away. Even then, only the outermost tape layer is affected; the reel must be unwound to get at the rest. Experts point out that simply spilling a cup of coffee on a disk or a tape is likely to be a more efficient weapon against magnetic data.

Some attacks against computers are extemporaneous, incited perhaps by momentary frustration or irritation with the victimized machines. But other assaults are planned and executed with cold-blooded precision by those who would attack society through its computers. Some incidents have caused great damage. For example, during the height of the Vietnam War, in 1970, American antiwar activists set off a bomb outside the Army Mathematics Research Center at the University of Wisconsin, killing a young graduate student working there after hours. By one estimate, the material losses—including buildings, computer hardware and a 20-year accumulation of research data—represented an investment of more than $18 million.

More recently, in Europe, terrorists armed variously with submachine guns, bombs and Molotov cocktails have mounted dozens of guerrilla-style assaults on computer installations. Unlike the attacks in the United States, these incidents extend beyond military or related targets to a broad array of civilian computer

A Mountain Fortress for Vital Computers

Perhaps the most thoroughly fortified computer facility in the world is the command post of the North American Aerospace Defense Command (NORAD), the binational mission charged with the air defense of the United States and Canada. More than 80 computers are buried in a subterranean city deep inside Colorado's Cheyenne Mountain. Cocooned by solid granite, the self-contained complex is built to withstand virtually any conceivable natural disaster or act of sabotage or war, barring a direct multimegaton nuclear strike.

In the early 1960s, more than 690,000 tons of rock were carved out of the mountain to create nearly three miles of interconnected tunnels and caverns. A roadway that runs east and west through the granite redoubt doubles as the central air-supply duct and is guarded around the clock. Massive, blastproof steel doors give entry from the roadway to a complex of 15 freestanding buildings occupying stone chambers that are 56 to 60 feet high. When the doors are shut, the only link to the outside is a deeply buried web of electronic communication cables.

Many of the details about the NORAD compound are secret. But on these and on the following two pages, an artist's renderings based on unclassified information illustrate some of the defenses that were developed to preserve this computer nerve center from physical harm.

Seventeen hundred feet beneath Cheyenne Mountain's rugged wilderness peak, the NORAD command post lies in a four-and-a-half-acre catacomb of granite caverns separated by huge pillars of intact rock. Four granite reservoirs and a 500,000-gallon diesel storage tank contain enough water and fuel to sustain the facility for 30 days.

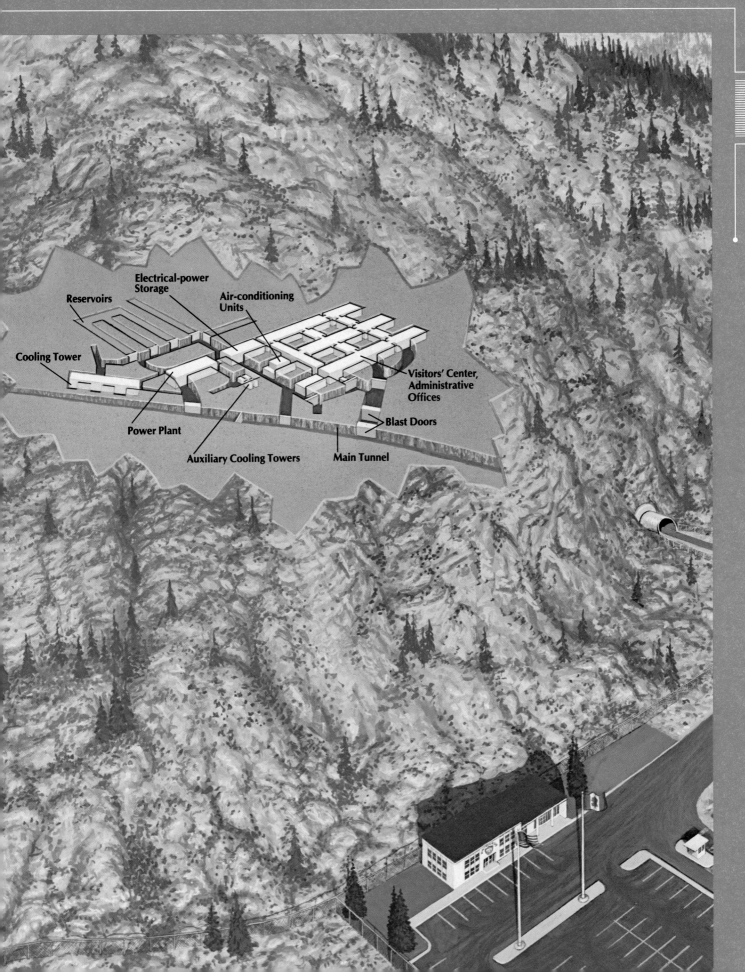

Reservoirs

Electrical-power
Storage

Air-conditioning
Units

Cooling Tower

Power Plant

Auxiliary Cooling Towers

Main Tunnel

Visitors' Center,
Administrative
Offices

Blast Doors

2

A Mountain Fortress for Vital Computers

A SHOCKPROOF STRUCTURE

Each building in the complex rests in its own granite cavern on steel springs that let the structure roll with any shock waves that penetrate the mountain; no part of the building touches the rock. Friction dampers, like giant shock absorbers, further reduce the shaking that could result from an earthquake or a nuclear explosion. Wire mesh on the walls protects communication and power cables from rockfalls. To counter the tendency of granite to shift under its own weight, expandable bolts, ranging in length from six to 32 feet, are inserted into the rockface to form a compressed layer that strengthens the walls of the caverns.

BLASTPROOF PORTALS

To enter the NORAD complex, a visitor must travel into the mountain on the main road and turn off to pass through a pair of three-foot-thick steel doors that weigh 25 tons apiece. The outer door is designed to close flush with the rock wall of the roadway, which is open at either end. The roadway thus acts to channel heat and percussion from an explosion through the mountain and away from the doors and the complex behind them.

guards flung open the mantrap doors and visually checked the identity cards of the employees filing past.

Embarrassing wrinkles of this sort usually get ironed out ahead of time by a thorough rehearsing of procedures and even by the staging of simulated assaults on the security system. In England, for example, a team of consultants that includes a former Scotland Yard detective specializes in computer-center break-ins. With the aid of hired actors who assume the role of intruder, the team probes for weaknesses in a center's protective armor.

The costs of all this safety—from special consultants to fortress-like construction and high-tech access control—can run into the millions of dollars at a large computer center. But an organization may get some of its investment back. One U.S. insurance company that recognizes the value of top-flight computer security reduces premiums for security-conscious clients by as much as half.

A MATTER OF TREACHERY
For all the money that is spent on protection, one aspect of computer security remains problematical. By far the most serious threat stems not from the intruders that tight security keeps out but from the ranks of trusted employees it is designed to let in: the programmers, operators, supervisors and others who service and maintain the computers.

These insiders commit an alarming number of computer crimes and abuses, in an astonishing variety of ways. At one extreme, they act out of political conviction. Terrorists' arson and bomb attacks against computer facilities in Europe often could not occur without the collusion of inside sympathizers. But more commonly, people assault computers for personal reasons. Sometimes the impetus may be simple frustration. In North Carolina, a computer operator became so exasperated with the machine that he pulled out a pistol and shot it. In the heavily guarded office of the U.S. Solicitor General in Washington, D.C., an unidentified insider once urinated on a computer.

Other insiders may strike out at the machines as a way of getting back at the boss. Belden Menkus, an independent security consultant, has related the tale of a computer-tape librarian at an insurance company in Hartford, Connecticut, who was having simultaneous affairs with two men in the data-processing division. This real-life soap opera stirred so much turmoil in the computer center that she was fired. While serving out her 30 days' notice, however, she took a librarian's revenge. Methodically, she began work on the data tapes in her charge, misfiling or mislabeling many of them. The rest of the tapes she erased with a degausser, a device that generates a strong magnetic field and is used in computer facilities for wiping unwanted data from old tapes before reusing or discarding them. The librarian's handiwork, which was not discovered until the day after her departure, threw the company's records into chaos. According to Menkus, "It cost the insurance company $10 million to recreate the data this woman had destroyed."

The standard measures for preventing insiders from abusing company computer systems or profiting from them—careful screening of job applicants, counseling for employees with personal problems, restriction of physical access to those who genuinely require it—provide some answers, but not all. In order to be certain that none of their computer specialists run amuck, employers would

Setting a Mantrap against Intruders

Protecting a facility from intruders requires verifying the identity of everyone seeking entry. In 1974, Dallas-based computer manufacturer Texas Instruments began routing access to its own data-processing center through a double-doored device known as a mantrap. Under the control of a computerized sentinel, the mantrap employs three separate verification techniques. Every authorized user of the facility is identified by an individual pass number and by two physical characteristics: voice and weight.

Upon enrollment in the system, a person repeats 16 different words into a device that translates the distinctive sound waves into digital form; this is stored as a template in the computer's memory (pages 46-47). At the same time, to give the computer a combination of identifying characteristics that would be difficult for an impostor to fake, the user's weight is recorded. The weight identification also prevents another person from trying to sneak through, or piggyback, on the valid access of an authorized user. If the weight is more than 40 pounds over the registered weight, the computer assumes that a second person is in the booth and signals for another pass number.

① After entering the identification booth, a user punches a pass number on a 12-button key pad, signaling the computer to retrieve the voice template and weight record registered by the person assigned that number.

② Through an overhead speaker, the computer broadcasts a four-word phrase randomly selected from the 16 words previously registered.

③ The user repeats the phrase into the microphone; the sounds are digitized for comparison with the record on file.

④ If the voice patterns match and the weight on the floor scale is no more than 40 pounds over the weight on record, the exit door leading into the data-processing center will automatically unlock. If a user is not verified after seven tries, a security officer investigates.

Turning Data into a Personal Template

Most biometric identification systems, whether they analyze a person's fingerprints, voice or signature, have certain features in common. For one thing, they usually require data from the real world—light or sound, for instance—to be converted into an information stream a computer can understand. As illustrated below, the computer receives a continuous flow of data from its sensors, in the form of an electrical signal that increases and decreases in voltage. In a system that uses fingerprints for identification, for example, the sensor will read the print's ridges as alternating areas of light and dark and will represent them as rising and falling voltage intensities.

The continuous electrical flow is called an analog signal; its

Providing data. In the first step, the user submits samples of the trait to be measured to a specialized sensor. For some systems the enrollee might provide speech or signature samples; in others the computer might record fingerprint, hand, or retina features.

Creating an analog signal. The data is converted to an electrical signal, with high and low voltages representing such traits as strong and weak acoustic power in a voice, heavy and light pressure in a signature, or bright and dark regions in an image.

Sampling. To convert the fluctuating but continuous analog signal into the computer's digital code, the computer samples the signal, isolating and measuring individual moments of the continuous flow.

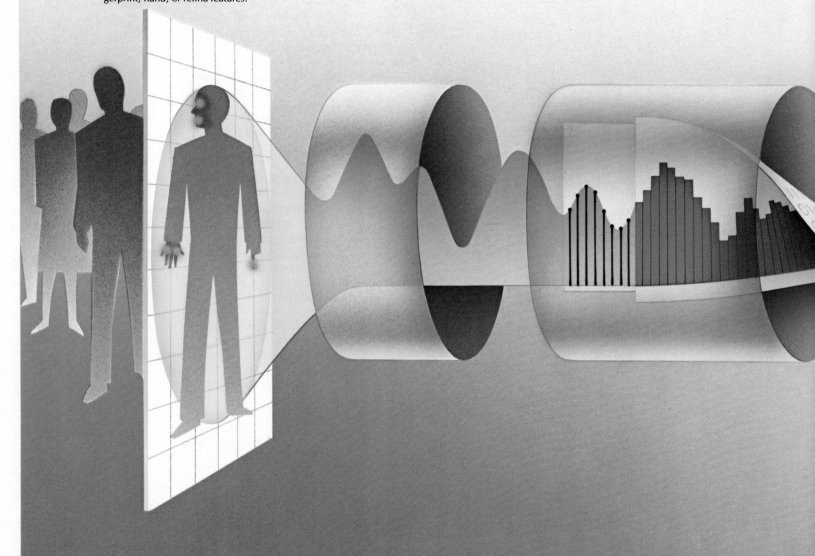

voltage changes serve as an analogy for nonelectrical changes in the real world. An analog-to-digital converter measures the voltage of the analog input hundreds of times a second, thereby dividing the continuous signal into a series of discrete signals called samples. Each sample is equivalent to one frame in a movie: By itself it represents only one frozen moment of input, but in sequence with other samples it makes a recognizable facsimile of the original continuous signal. The computer then assigns a numerical value to each sample and stores those numbers as binary digits, or bits.

In practice, minor variations occur from one time to the next when a person is inspected by a biometric security system. No signature is duplicated exactly each time it is signed; the voice can change with age, sickness and stress; and a fingerprint's impression may be smeared, placed off-center or partially obscured. Thus, at the time a new user is enrolled, most systems follow a procedure that will allow for some variations in the future. Instead of making only one initial reading, the system takes several. These are then manipulated according to a formula to create an electronic template of the identifying characteristic. Then, when the user's identity must be verified later, the computer is given a prescribed amount of leeway before having to reject a sample for not being a close enough match.

Digitizing the signal. The computer assigns each sample a numerical value within a prescribed range and translates the values into the form of the binary digits one and zero; the computer reads the bits as a sequence of on-off electronic pulses.

Processing. The digitized signal is processed by an algorithm, a set of instructions in the system's software that manipulates the binary digits, often condensing them for the most efficient storage.

Making the template. Usually, to allow for minor variations, several readings of an identifying trait are taken and then merged mathematically. The result is an electronic ID the system can refer to every time the enrolled user seeks access.

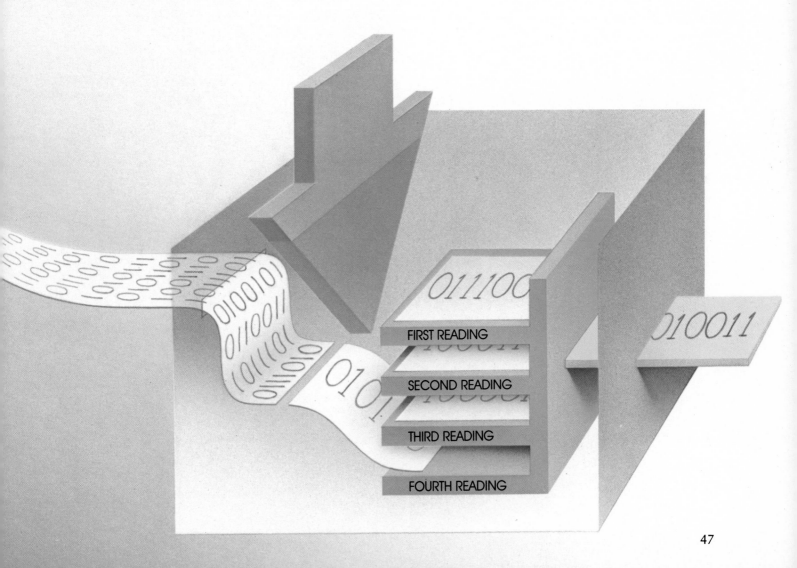

FIRST READING

SECOND READING

THIRD READING

FOURTH READING

Measuring the Act of Writing

A user at a remote terminal signs for access to a multi-user computer system. A signature template stored in the central computer verifies the signer's identity.

Sensors for Three Signals

This biometric pen converts a signature into a set of three electrical signals by means of piezoelectric transducers, ceramic devices that generate measurable voltages in response to stress. One transducer senses changes in the writer's downward pressure on the penpoint; farther up the pen shaft, two transducers set at right angles to each other measure vertical and horizontal movement. Although the computer does not need a visible signature, the pen also includes an ink cartridge; tests have shown that people sign more naturally if they see what they are writing.

Pressure Sensor

Acceleration Sensors

Thomas Worthington

When human observers verify a signature, they normally concentrate on the way the name looks. A biometric verification system takes a different measure, judging a signature not by its appearance but by the dynamics of the signing process—the changes in force as the writer's hand touches down lightly for one stroke, harder on the next.

The system's sensors may be incorporated into a sensitive pad on which the signature is written, or they may be built into the signing pen. The verification pen illustrated here was developed by a team of IBM scientists directed by Thomas Worthington, whose signature is used in this explanation. Typically, the pen is attached by a flexible cable to a terminal that is part of a multi-user system.

Signals from the pen's sensors are translated into a trio of electrical wave forms, one representing changes in downward pressure, the other two representing acceleration along the pen's vertical and horizontal axes. The crossing of a *t*, for example, would register as a high point in the horizontal and a low point in the vertical wave form, whereas the dotting of an *i* would produce a peak in the pressure-change wave while leaving both of the acceleration wave forms relatively flat. A curved or diagonal stroke, for its part, would generate action in both acceleration signals.

To become enrolled in the signature verification system, a person typically writes six signatures, from which the computer chooses two samples to make a verification template. Later, when the enrollee seeks access to the system, the computer will request the person's identification number, retrieve the appropriate verification template from memory, then ask for a signature. Only if the dynamics of the signature match those of the template closely enough will the computer allow the person access to the system.

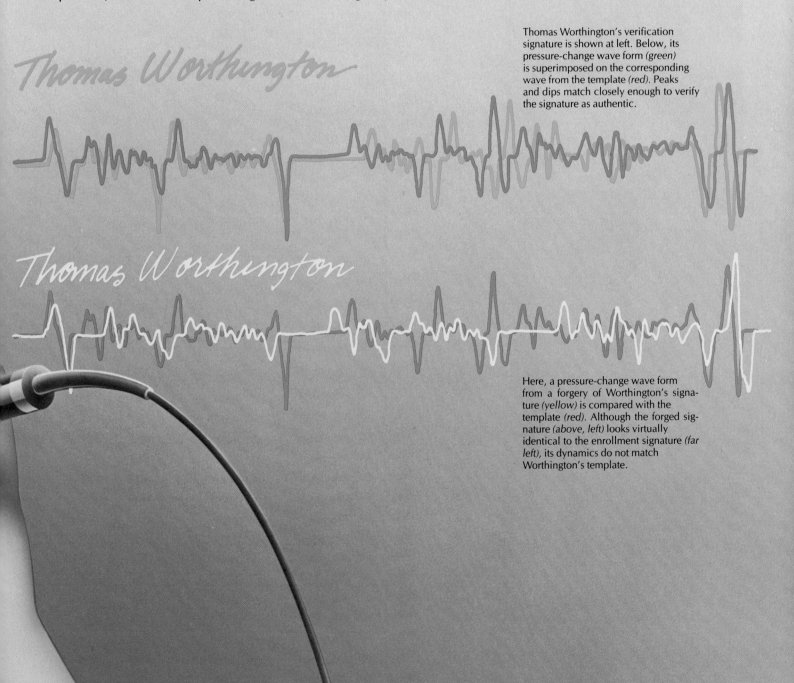

Thomas Worthington's verification signature is shown at left. Below, its pressure-change wave form *(green)* is superimposed on the corresponding wave from the template *(red)*. Peaks and dips match closely enough to verify the signature as authentic.

Here, a pressure-change wave form from a forgery of Worthington's signature *(yellow)* is compared with the template *(red)*. Although the forged signature *(above, left)* looks virtually identical to the enrollment signature *(far left)*, its dynamics do not match Worthington's template.

The Individuality of a Vocal Signature

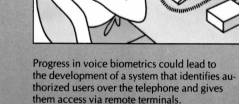

Progress in voice biometrics could lead to the development of a system that identifies authorized users over the telephone and gives them access via remote terminals.

October Ninth
Nineteen Seventy

The waveform below indicates the fluctuating signal generated by the spoken phrase (a date memorable to the user). The spectrogram *(bottom)* pinpoints unique formants by graphing component frequencies.

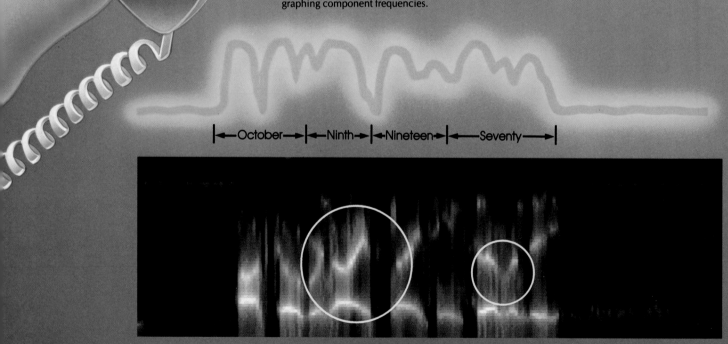

Largely still in the experimental stage, reliable computer systems for voice verification would be useful for both on-site and remote user identification. The voice verifier described here is a developmental system at American Telephone and Telegraph. Enrollment would require the user to repeat a particular phrase several times. The computer would sample, digitize and store each reading of the phrase and then, from the data, build a voice signature that would make allowances for an individual's characteristic variations.

For purposes of analysis, the computer first focuses mainly on the simplest characteristic of a voice: its acoustic strength. This fluctuates during a spoken phrase from silence to varying degrees of loudness. To isolate personal characteristics within these fluctuations, the computer breaks the sound into its component frequencies and analyzes how they are distributed. On a spectrogram—a visual representation of the voice *(bottom)*—the high-amplitude frequencies are indicated by bright spots called formants. The precise appearance of the formants is determined by the unique shape and movement of a speaker's lips, tongue, throat and vocal cords.

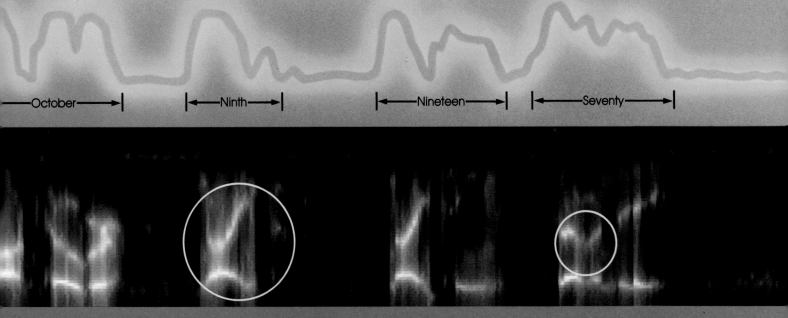

Oc-to-ber . . . Nin-th . . . Nine-teen . . . Se-ven-ty . . .

Even when the speaker deliberately draws out the phrase, the characteristic formants of the voice signature remain constant electronic diagrams of the unique configurations of the speaker's mouth and vocal cords.

|←—October—→| |←—Ninth—→| |←—Nineteen—→| |←—Seventy—→|

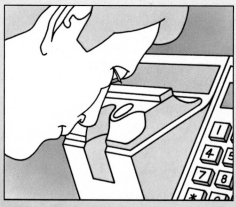

Patterns in the Eye

To enroll in the system or to verify identity, the user looks into an eyepiece, focuses on a designated point behind the lens and receives a low-intensity infrared scan.

An infrared sensor in the scanning device perceives blood vessels as a da pattern against lighter retinal tissue. A microprocessor in the unit digitizes this image by assigning a numerical value—from zero for the darkest gra to 4,095 for the lightest—to each of 320 sampled points.

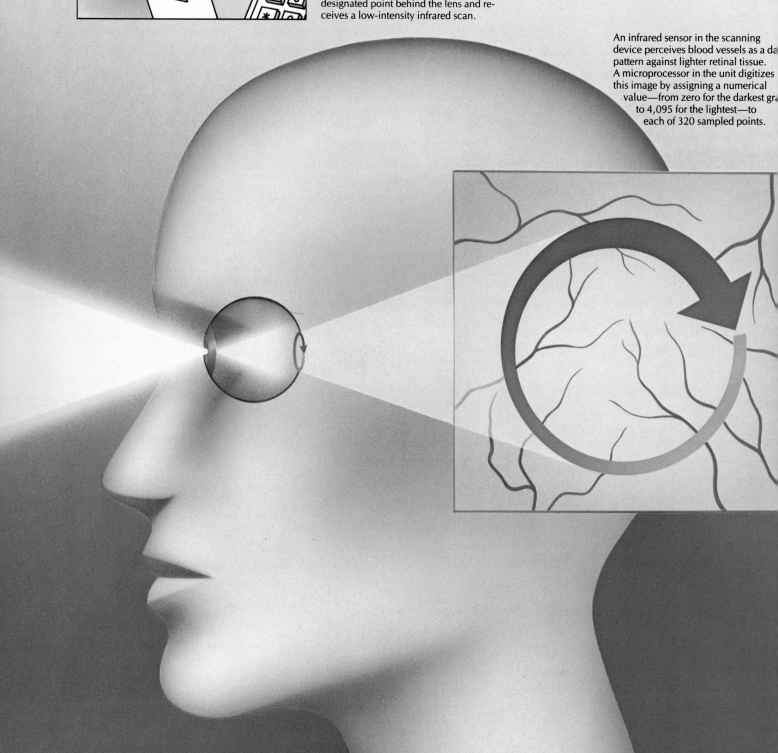

Every person carries at the back of each eyeball a pattern as distinct and inimitable as a fingerprint. But unlike a fingerprint, the fine tracery of blood vessels in the retinal tissue is an invisible identifier that cannot be recorded manually. It cannot even be photographed with an ordinary camera.

The biometric identification system illustrated on these pages uses an infrared beam, which scans the retina in a circular path. A detector in the eyepiece of the device measures the intensity of the light as it is reflected from different points. Because blood vessels do not absorb and reflect the same quantities of infrared as the surrounding tissue, the eyepiece sensor records the vessels as an intricate dark pattern against a lighter background. The device samples light intensity at 320 points around the path of the scan, producing a digital profile of the vessel pattern. (Only one inspection is necessary, since a person's retinaprint, or retinal signature, does not change as the voice or a written signature does.) The algorithm in the system's software then compresses the digital profile into a reference template.

Enrollment can take as little as 30 seconds and verification can be even faster: The user types in an identification number to call up the reference template from the computer's memory and then looks into the eyepiece for a retinal scan. In only a second and a half, the computer compares the scan results with the template and grants access if the two signatures are a close enough match.

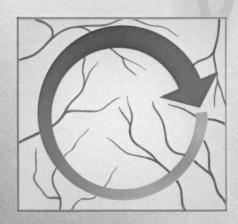

The retina-pattern template from the eye at left and opposite can be drawn as a waveform (above), with peaks for the brightest areas of the image and valleys for the darkest. The computer creates the template by manipulating the digitized scan data according to a formula and storing the result in memory as a sequence of binary digits.

The image at left represents another—and markedly different—retinal pattern, and its waveform signature reflects that difference. Manufacturers of this system assert that when the system is set to accurate specifications it will let an unauthorized user through only one time in a million.

Recording the Geometry of the Hand

Schoolchildren who trace their hands in art class quickly discover that no two are exactly alike. Shown here is a biometric security system that uses this principle to verify an individual's identity. Instead of a sketch, the system employs a sophisticated scanning device to record the unique measurements of each person's hand.

A user enrolls in a so-called hand geometry system by placing one hand on the metal plate of a reading device, positioning the middle and ring fingers on either side of a small peg and aligning all the fingers along narrow grooves slotted with glass (right). An overhead light shines down on the hand, and a sensor underneath the plate scans the fingers through the glass slots, recording light intensity from the fingertips to the webbing where the fingers join the palm. The device measures each finger to within 1/10,000 of an inch, marking where the finger begins and ends by the varying intensities of light. The information is digitized and stored in the system as a template or coded on a magnetic-strip ID card.

Despite the uniqueness of individual hands, hand geometry identification is not foolproof. For example, if a user with long fingernails enrolled in the system wearing heavy nail polish, the sensor could not detect the true ends of the fingertips, which would be hidden by the dark nails. The computer would thus be unable to verify the person's identity if she tried to gain access after removing the nail polish.

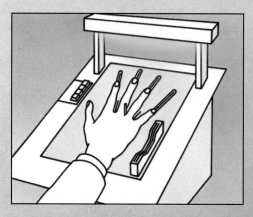

With light shining from above, a sensor beneath the metal plate scans the user's hand, taking measurements of the light intensity of each finger from tip to palm.

C

D

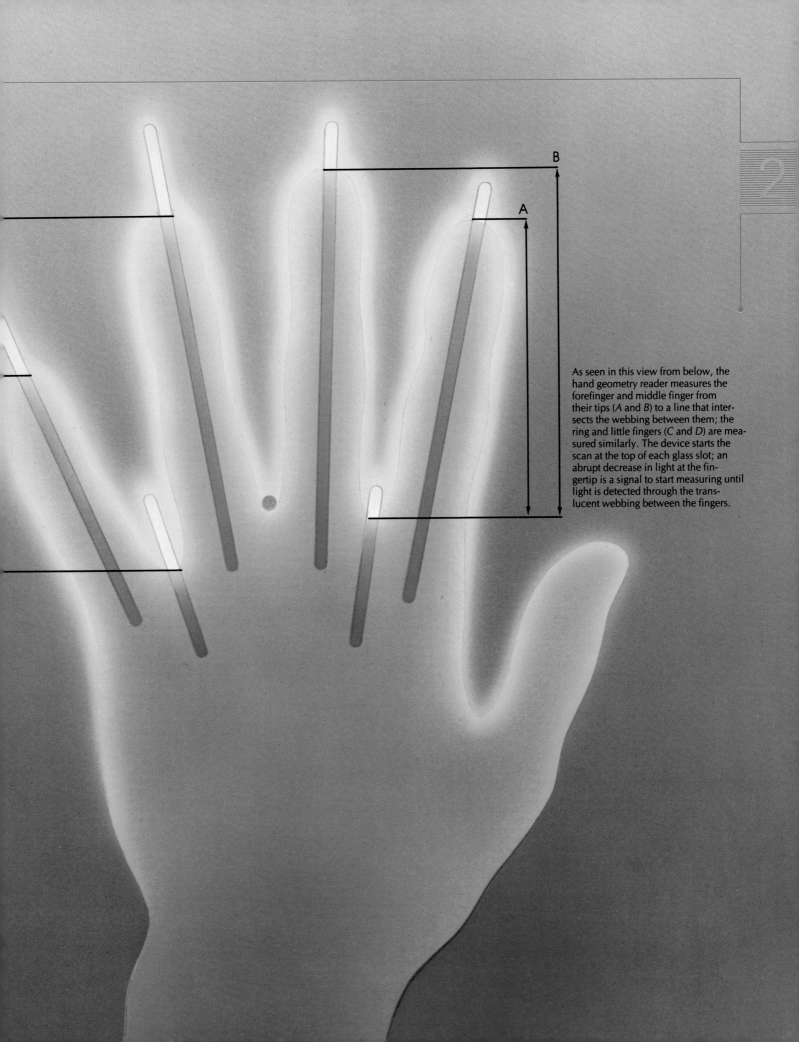

As seen in this view from below, the hand geometry reader measures the forefinger and middle finger from their tips (*A* and *B*) to a line that intersects the webbing between them; the ring and little fingers (*C* and *D*) are measured similarly. The device starts the scan at the top of each glass slot; an abrupt decrease in light at the fingertip is a signal to start measuring until light is detected through the translucent webbing between the fingers.

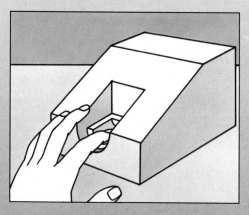

Mapping the Intricacies of a Fingerprint

In a fingerprint verification system, the user places one finger on a glass plate; light flashes inside the machine, reflects off the fingerprint and is picked up by an optical scanner. The scanner transmits the information to the computer for analysis.

At the core of the print, data from each pixel (its numerical gray-scale value) is fed into an algorithm that analyzes clusters of pixels to determine where ridge splits and endings occur (*marked here by red patches*).

The system is designed to focus on one square inch (*below*), centered on the core of the print (*shown enlarged at right*). The computer samples data from this area on a grid of 500 by 500 picture elements, or pixels.

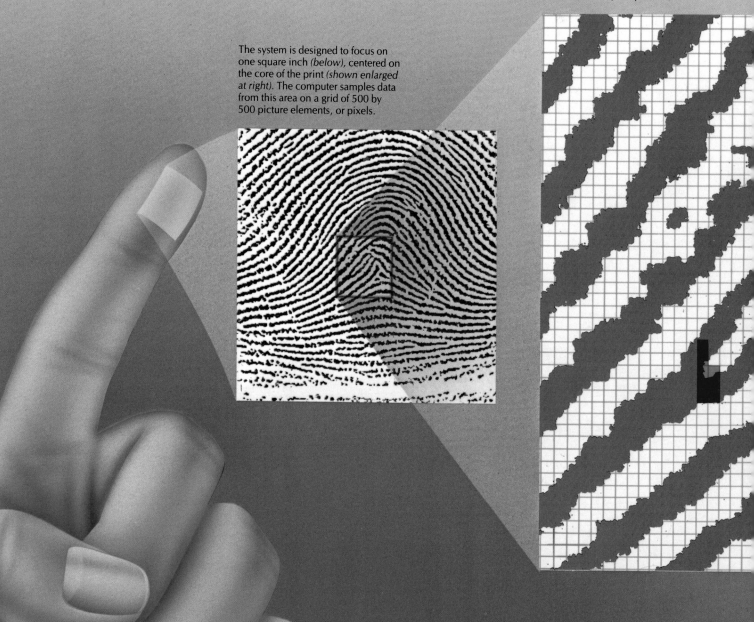

Fingerprint identification is based on the anatomical truth that no two fingerprints are exactly alike; each has a unique pattern of prominent features such as arches, loops and whorls. But trying to identify an individual print from these characteristics alone is often problematic. If a print's impression is smudged or distorted by dirt, for instance, the patterns may be sufficiently incomplete to make a positive identification impossible. With the advent of computerized fingerprint systems, security experts can now verify identity by looking at so-called minutiae, smaller details and variations within the larger features.

At enrollment, data samples from a scan of the user's fingerprint are interpreted as varying degrees of gray and assigned a numerical value. This gray-scale representation is processed by a complex algorithm, which pays special attention to the places where clusters of light and dark points indicate that a ridge has divided or ended. The system is designed to analyze these minute ridge splits and endings, ascertaining their positions relative to the core of the print and to one another; the system also analyzes the angle of the ridges. These relationships remain unaltered even when a print's impression is faint, dirty or distorted.

Several readings are taken and manipulated by the algorithm to create a stored template. A user wishing to gain access to a secure area merely enters an identification number to call up the template, places the same finger in the scanner and waits a few seconds for a verification analysis. If the prints are a close enough match, access is granted.

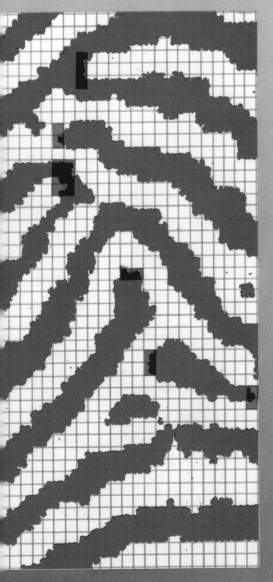

The system can read even a fingerprint that is partially illegible because of dirt, injury or insufficient pressure on the scanner. The faint print at right is from the same finger as the one at far left; the machine can recognize it by the relative positions of its minutiae.

Frequently the system has to read prints that are askew. Here, the print scanned for verification is not aligned as it was at enrollment. Despite the altered orientation of the lines, however, the distinctive placement of the minutiae remains unchanged.

Trojan Horses
and Logic Bombs

Richard Streeter, a CBS Inc. executive and computer hobbyist in Fanwood, New Jersey, retired to his recreation room one summer day in 1985 to pursue a favorite diversion: checking electronic bulletin boards for new computer programs free for the taking. On this day, he used the modem attached to his computer to dial a bulletin board operated by an acquaintance on Long Island.

Streeter availed himself of a bulletin-board feature that displayed on his monitor only programs posted since he had last logged on. One offering caught his eye. As Streeter recalled several months later, the program, EGABTR, "promised to improve by 50 percent" the performance of a computer-graphics circuit board he had recently purchased. Intrigued, Streeter copied the program onto his own computer's main-storage disk drive, a capacious device capable of holding 30 million bytes of information. Then he tried out the program.

Reflecting on what happened next, Streeter felt that he might have been more alert to trouble. EGABTR came without instructions, an ominous sign. And the program asked that a disk be slipped into an auxiliary disk drive attached to his machine, something that should have been unnecessary for a graphics-enhancing program. Streeter complied, only to be greeted by an insolent message on the monitor: "Arf, arf! Got you!" Streeter found out what "Got you!" meant when he tried to retrieve information from his storage disks. Nothing was there. EGABTR had effectively destroyed more than 900 computer programs and documents by scrambling the computer's index to the files. Without the index, the information might as well never have existed.

EGABTR is an example of what computer-security specialists refer to as a Trojan horse. Much as warriors of ancient Greece hid inside a wooden horse presented to the city of Troy as a peace offering, a small computer program is concealed among the thousands—or even millions—of lines of instructions that constitute an otherwise legitimate piece of software. Then, when the software is running on the computer, the secret instructions lurking inside spring into action. Like the Greek soldiers who spilled out of the horse and opened the gates of Troy to the army laying siege to the city, the computer-age Trojan horse begins performing unexpected functions.

The Trojan horse and similar techniques are all-purpose tools for attacking the computer. They enable people to recruit the computer itself as an accomplice in crimes ranging from fraud to outright sabotage. Such offenses, which involve the electronic manipulation of data or programs, typically are staged so stealthily that they may go undetected for months or years. "Computer crime is a low-visibility proposition," a U.S. Department of Justice official told a Senate committee in a report submitted in 1976. "There are no smoking pistols—no blood-stained victims; often the crime is detected by sheer accident."

Since that warning, computerized attacks on computers have grown more frequent, and the attacks themselves have become more sophisticated. In addition, the potential for wrongdoing swells as more and more people gain access to

In the hands of dishonest computer operators and programmers, a computer system can undergo a disturbing metamorphosis. One moment it is an obedient servant; the next it contains a hidden serpent that can steal data, ruin programs and even bring the system crashing to a halt.

designated when he placed his order. Letting himself through the gate with a key sold to him by a friend who recently had quit the telephone company, Schneider picked up his order. For an illusion of legitimacy, he forged on each piece of equipment the telephone-company stamp "Released for Resale," then delivered the goods to his waiting clients. Later, after discovering the level of inventory at which the PT&T computer automatically reordered, Schneider even began re-selling the telephone company its own equipment. It was a simple matter for him to requisition an item until PT&T's supply was sufficiently depleted, then offer his stock to the company as replenishment.

According to Schneider, over a period of seven months, he fleeced PT&T's inventory computer of nearly one million dollars. He established his own ware-house, staffed by 10 employees, whom he kept in the dark about the source of the equipment. But the strain of running a business by day, a racket in the wee hours of the morning and attending classes at night began to tell. He confided in one of his employees and recruited his help in handling the clandestine pickups. But after Schneider refused the fellow's request for a $40-a-week raise, the employee turned him in. In 1972 Schneider struck a bargain with the prosecution. He pleaded guilty to grand theft, paid PT&T a mere $8,500 in restitution and served 40 days in jail, where he helped Los Angeles County develop a computerized inventory-control system. Then, at the age of 23, he went into business as a security consultant, helping companies safeguard their computers against the likes of Jerry Schneider.

INSTANT RICHES FROM THE BANKING SYSTEM

During the decade after Schneider's caper, the spread of so-called electronic money rendered such elaborate and exhausting frauds unnecessary. As banks and other financial institutions came to depend upon electronic funds transfers (EFTs), new opportunities arose. With just a minute or two at the keyboard, a data diddler can use a computer to manipulate enormous sums of money over long-distance telephone wires.

A nimble con artist once staged just such a crime with the unwitting collusion of his girlfriend, a data-processing clerk at a West Coast bank. First, the man opened an account at a New York bank, posing as a furniture manufacturer who was transferring money from his West Coast account to finance a new plant in the East. Then he persuaded his girlfriend to type into the computer an order transmit-ting two million dollars from her employer to the New York account, explaining it as a practical joke on a computer-operator friend at the New York end of the line; the friend would understand the message as a fake, the con man said, and enjoy the charade. But as soon as the deposit was credited to the New York account, the swindler collected the two million dollars and disappeared.

Had the thief allied himself with a computer programmer, his take might have been even greater, and at less risk of discovery. Expert programmers can often contrive a more inconspicuous entry into a computer system: They can search for an opening known as a trap door. A typical trap door is a set of special instruc-tions written into a computer's operating system—or some other program—that allows a systems manager to bypass normal security procedures to test the soft-ware before the system becomes operational. These special codes are usually erased and the trap doors closed before the computer is put to use, but sometimes they are overlooked or purposely left behind to ease maintenance, including upgrading or troubleshooting. In that event, the trap door invites abuse, enabling an intruder to enter sensitive files.

The idea that this kind of loophole can exist even in supposedly secure systems was given wide currency in the popular movie *WarGames*. In that film, the designer of a vital Department of Defense computer program creates a trap door that springs open in response to the password "Joshua." After the designer mysteriously disappears, a young hacker discovers the Joshua trap door, opens it and inadvertently sets in motion a simulated war game that threatens to culminate in actual global nuclear warfare.

In real life, computer criminals have taken advantage of existing trap doors for profit. A group of automotive engineers in Detroit once discovered such an opening after dialing into a Florida time-sharing service. Through the trap door they found the password of the service's president and thus gained entry into important proprietary software, which they proceeded to copy and use free of charge. When trap doors do not already exist, hackers have created them just for

Disk anatomy. Before a disk can be used, it must be formatted—divided into concentric tracks and wedgelike sectors. A disk directory keeps tabs on the sector and track coordinates of the pieces of a file, which may be scattered all over the disk.

Directory shift. If the disk directory *(red in outer tracks)* is moved from its usual location, files on a copied disk will be inaccessible; the instructions telling the computer where the directory is cannot be copied by normal copy commands.

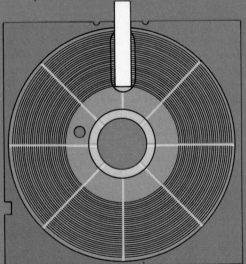

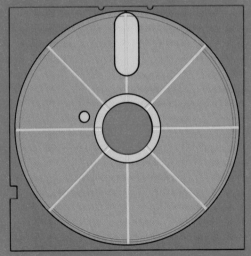

A so-called index hole through the disk's jacket and the disk itself enables the disk drive's read-write head *(white)* to orient itself by finding the first sector and track. The head makes contact with selected portions of the disk through the slot opening in the jacket.

Instead of using standard copy commands, a programmer could instruct the computer to copy data from one disk to another by naming sector and track coordinates. Activating these commands requires that the pirate be well versed in the computer's operating system.

fun. Having broken into a computer system via modem, a hacker leaves behind a set of special instructions that provides future access.

In either case, once the walls have been breached, the versatile Trojan horse is an ideal tool for automating crimes such as embezzlement. To avoid arousing suspicions, embezzlers sometimes use a Trojan horse technique that security experts call the salami method—slicing ill-gotten gains into increments thin enough to go unnoticed. A bank's computer programmer, for example, could conceivably enjoy a handsome extra income by instructing the computer to subtract automatically and randomly, under the guise of service charges, 10 or 15 cents a month from many of the checking accounts it processes and then divert the funds into a dummy account. Or a programmer might profit from the fractions of pennies that result from interest calculations on savings-account deposits. Instead of having the computer distribute these individually insignificant amounts equitably among all accounts, the programmer might channel them to a single account under a false name. Customers would be unlikely to complain; none would lose more than pennies at a time. And auditors might never dis-

Altered checksums. Checksums, results of mathematical operations on the bits in a sector, are used to verify accuracy when a disk is used. Incorrect checksums are put in some sectors of protected software; instructions stop operations if the errors are corrected, as occurs when a disk is copied.

Half tracks. Some systems use so-called half tracks between the tracks a disk drive usually reads or writes data on. A program on the half tracks *(below, red)* must also have instructions (which cannot be copied with standard commands) telling the computer how to reposition the drive heads.

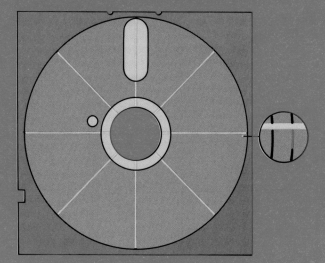

A pirate who can program in low-level assembly language can remove the instructions to look for incorrect checksums or write instructions telling the computer to copy the disk exactly, errors and all.

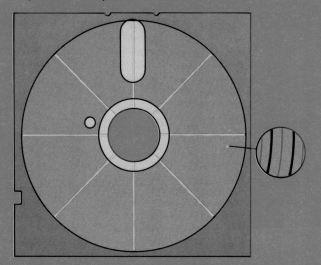

Circumventing this protection method requires programming expertise. A pirate who is familiar with both assembly language and the workings of disk-drive hardware can write a program to reposition the drive heads to read the copied disk.

cover the embezzlement because, overall, the bank's books would balance.

Trojan horses do not all operate so subtly. Some of them, like the EGABTR program that destroyed computer hobbyist Richard Streeter's data, go off with a bang. Indeed, they are known among security specialists as logic bombs. EGABTR had a short fuse, exploding the first time it was used. More often, logic bombs are set to detonate under a particular set of conditions or, like a time bomb, at a specified moment in the future. The extent of the damage depends on the instructions. A logic bomb exploding in the Los Angeles department of water and power simply froze all of the computer's internal files, preventing anyone from using them. A French programmer, after being cashiered, left a farewell salute in the record-keeping software he had been working on. The bomb exploded two years later on New Year's Day, wiping out all the records stored on tape. Other programmers have altered software instructions to delete all names on a company's payroll if their own disappeared from the list.

On rare occasions, when a logic bomb is discovered before it detonates, it can point directly to the culprit, as an American graduate student once discovered.

Ambiguous bits. A disk may be physically altered so that the computer reads designated bits sometimes as ones, sometimes as zeros. A normal copy program cannot reproduce these ambiguous bits; it writes a one or a zero. Software can be designed not to work if ambiguous bits are missing.

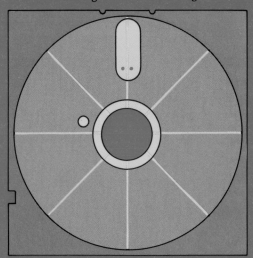

As with most other copy-protection methods, one way to bypass this scheme is to manipulate the original program at the assembly-language level, removing the instructions that tell the computer to look for ambiguous bits in the first place.

Hardware key. One way to protect a program is to put only part of it on a disk, and the rest into a microchip that plugs into the computer through a connecting device. The chip and the device act like a key to unlock the software; without it, the program on a pirated disk will not run.

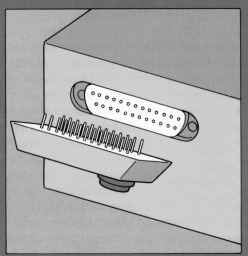

Dividing a program between a disk and a chip might stymie some copiers, but determined software pirates working in assembly language could eventually program their way around this protection system.

Gaining Admission to a Multi-User System

In most large multi-user computer systems, everyone who wishes to work on the computer, whether to type a memo or to enter new information into an existing data base, must first go through a start-up procedure called logging on or logging in, regardless of any security measures that may come into play later. The procedure, controlled by a program in the computer's operating system, either confirms a user's identity and attendant rights to enter the system, or denies access to an

To log onto his company's multi-user computer system, Bob, a salesperson, types his name at the keyboard of his terminal. This signals the operating system that he wants access to the computer. The operating system fetches the names-and-passwords file into temporary memory, finds Bob's name as an authorized user, and displays a password request. When Bob types in his secret password, the operating system determines that it matches the one on file with Bob's name, and he is given access to the system.

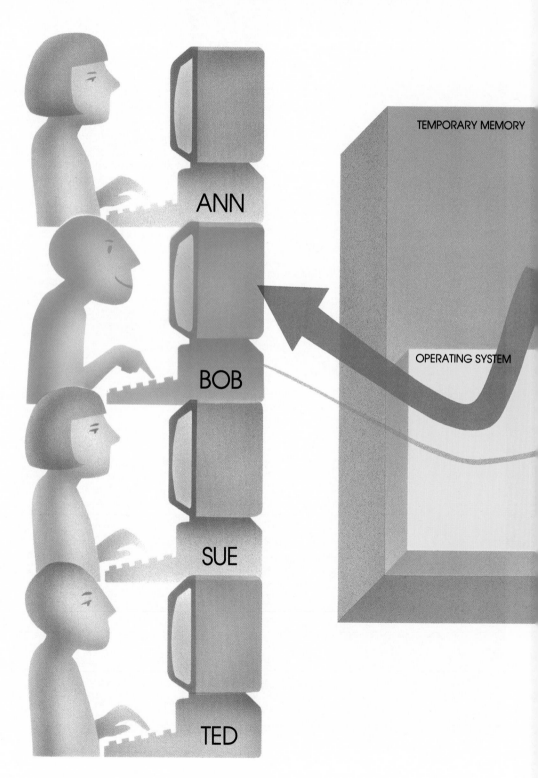

unauthorized person. Not only does the log-on procedure screen would-be users on the premises, it can also foil automated long-distance hacker attacks by rigorously limiting the number of unsuccessful attempts permitted per telephone call *(page 21)*.

In the sample system shown here and on the following pages, four employees are entitled to varying degrees of access to their company's computer system. In order for them to be able to operate such workday applications as the text-edit program, for instance, or to take a look at specific data, they must call that program or data file from storage on a tape or disk into the computer's temporary memory. All such requests for computerized files are made by way of the operating system, which will carry out only those requests made by users whose identity has been established during the log-on procedure.

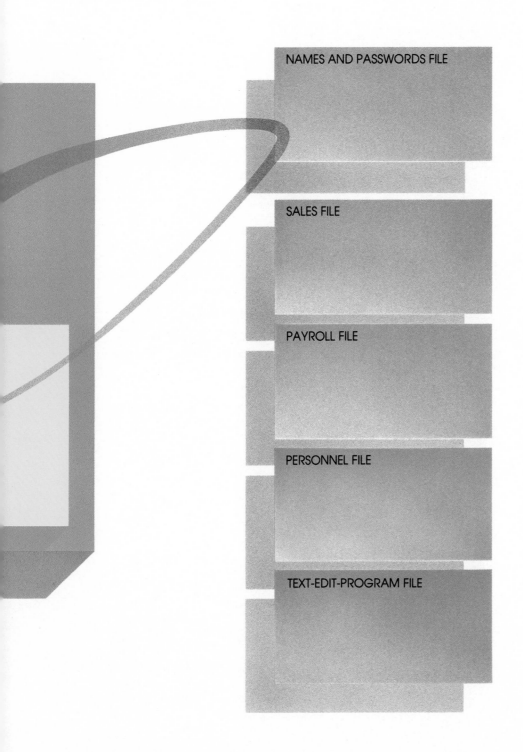

NAMES AND PASSWORDS FILE

SALES FILE

PAYROLL FILE

PERSONNEL FILE

TEXT-EDIT-PROGRAM FILE

Controlling Access to Computer Files

A simple method of regulating the security of electronic files is to head each one with a kind of shield known as an access-control list (ACL). An ACL names those authorized to use a file and specifies what kind of access each person is permitted. So-called read-access allows an individual to use a program or to look at the contents of a file but does not grant the right to alter the program or file in any way; to make additions, deletions or other changes, a user must also have write-access.

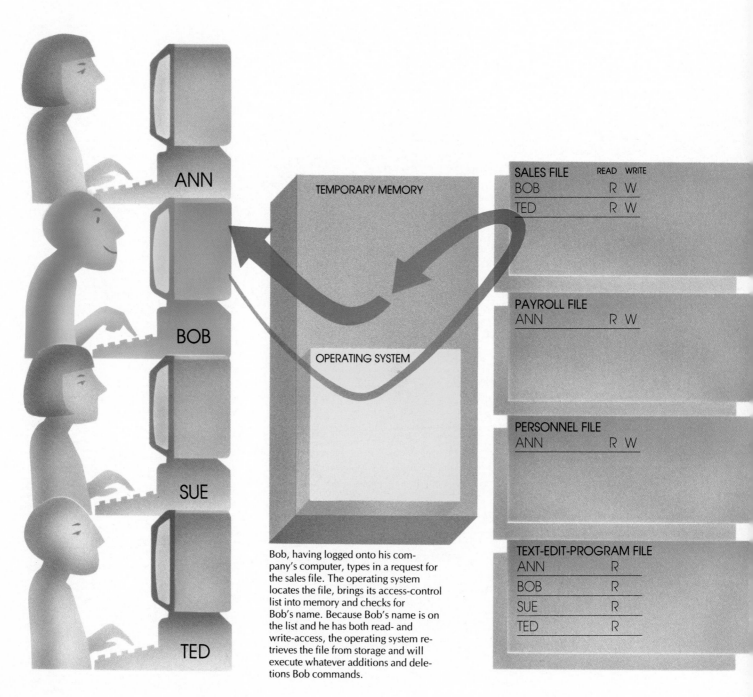

Bob, having logged onto his company's computer, types in a request for the sales file. The operating system locates the file, brings its access-control list into memory and checks for Bob's name. Because Bob's name is on the list and he has both read- and write-access, the operating system retrieves the file from storage and will execute whatever additions and deletions Bob commands.

SALES FILE	READ	WRITE
BOB	R	W
TED	R	W

PAYROLL FILE		
ANN	R	W

PERSONNEL FILE		
ANN	R	W

TEXT-EDIT-PROGRAM FILE		
ANN	R	
BOB	R	
SUE	R	
TED	R	

TEMPORARY MEMORY

OPERATING SYSTEM

ANN

BOB

SUE

TED

When the operating system receives a request for a file, it must first bring the relevant ACL into temporary memory to check for the user's name; only if the name is found will the file itself be brought into memory.

As indicated by the ACLs of the sample files below, an employee's access varies from file to file. Ann, a high-level executive, has both read- and write-access to the payroll and personnel files, allowing her the ability to add bonuses or adjust salaries. (Company accountants, on the other hand, might be given only read-access, allowing them merely to audit payroll records.) Salesperson Bob and sales manager Ted each have both read- and write-access to the sales file; either of them can update those records. Sue, the company secretary, has not been given access to any of the data files but does have read-access to the text-edit-program file for word processing, as does everyone else.

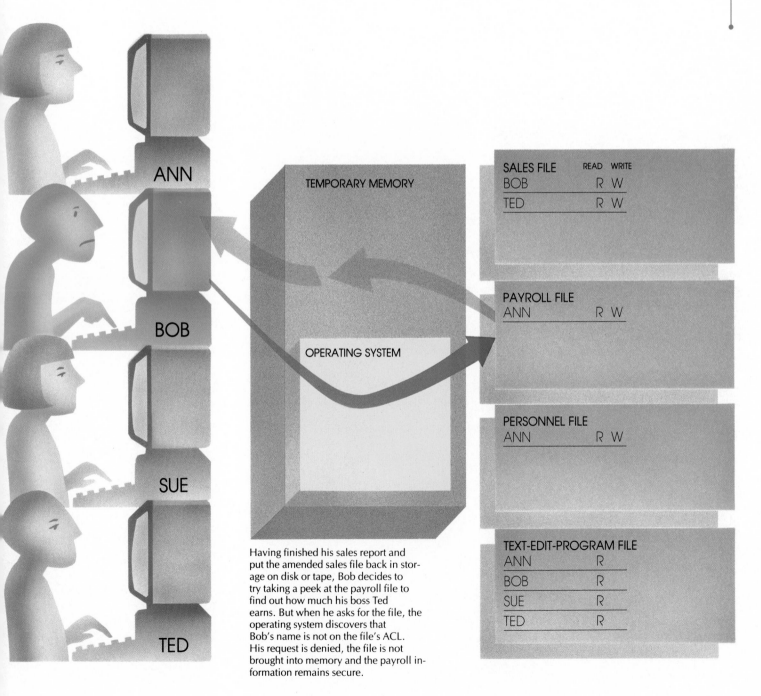

ANN

BOB

SUE

TED

TEMPORARY MEMORY

OPERATING SYSTEM

SALES FILE	READ	WRITE
BOB	R	W
TED	R	W

PAYROLL FILE		
ANN	R	W

PERSONNEL FILE		
ANN	R	W

TEXT-EDIT-PROGRAM FILE	
ANN	R
BOB	R
SUE	R
TED	R

Having finished his sales report and put the amended sales file back in storage on disk or tape, Bob decides to try taking a peek at the payroll file to find out how much his boss Ted earns. But when he asks for the file, the operating system discovers that Bob's name is not on the file's ACL. His request is denied, the file is not brought into memory and the payroll information remains secure.

Sneaking Data from Restricted Files

A system that relies principally on access-control lists for security can provide an effective safeguard against casual attempts to enter sensitive files. However, an ACL security system is vulnerable to a Trojan horse, a seemingly innocent piece of software that conceals within its code malicious instructions that deceive the computer and cause it to open confidential files. To carry out a Trojan horse attack, an unauthorized user first buries a request for restricted data inside some other program. The would-be trespasser then induces an authorized user to run the program and—all unknowingly—activate the request for restricted data. Shown below are the steps Bob undertakes to prepare a Trojan horse invasion of the payroll file.

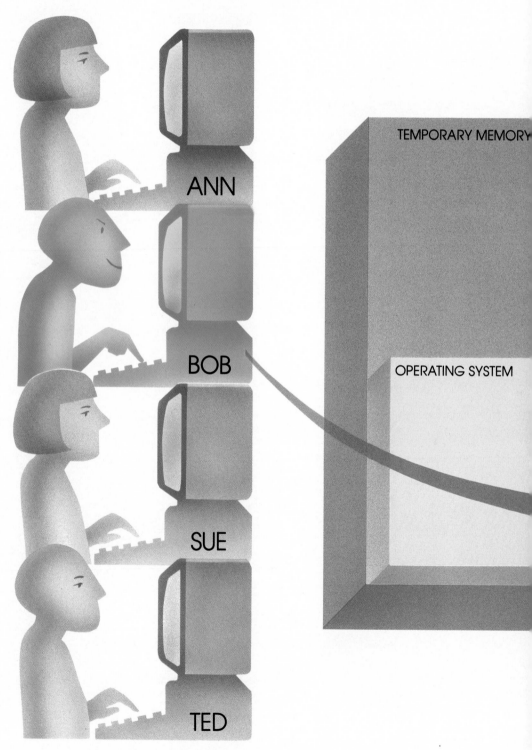

To build a Trojan horse, Bob first creates two new files, Bob's text-edit file and Bob's secret file, heading each one with an ACL that gives him both read- and write-access (1). He also gives Ann, who has access to the payroll file, read-access to Bob's text-edit file and write-access to Bob's secret file. Next, Bob copies the company's text-edit-program file into Bob's text-edit file (2): His read-access to the text-edit program allows him to copy it.

Because he has given himself write-access to the new file, Bob is now free to alter the copy. He writes two new sets of instructions (3). The first set automatically adjusts each page of text to make room for footnotes—a helpful feature designed to entice Ann into using the altered program. The second set of instructions is the secret one: It amends the text-edit program so that as soon as Ann activates it, the operating system will be asked to copy the payroll file into Bob's secret file.

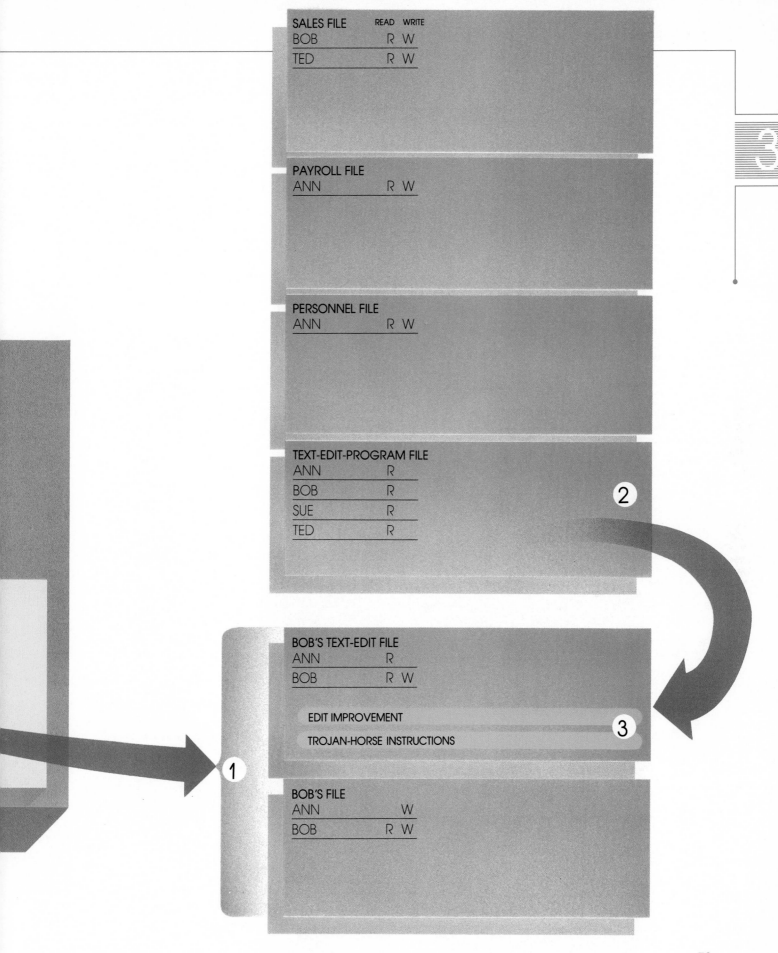

SALES FILE

	READ	WRITE
BOB	R	W
TED	R	W

PAYROLL FILE

ANN	R	W

PERSONNEL FILE

ANN	R	W

TEXT-EDIT-PROGRAM FILE

ANN	R
BOB	R
SUE	R
TED	R

BOB'S TEXT-EDIT FILE

ANN	R	
BOB	R	W

EDIT IMPROVEMENT

TROJAN-HORSE INSTRUCTIONS

BOB'S FILE

ANN		W
BOB	R	W

To put his Trojan horse into action, Bob shows Ann the new footnote feature in the word-processing program he has stored as Bob's text-edit file and convinces her that it is an improvement over the company's version.

Ann requests Bob's program the next time she does word processing; since she has been given read-access to the file, the operating system complies. Ann uses the new program, unaware that she is activating the Trojan horse and telling the computer to copy the restricted payroll file into Bob's newly created secret file, which he can read at will.

Such a command from Bob would be refused; but Ann, who seems to be making the request, has read-access to the payroll file, so the operating system perceives the command as legitimate.

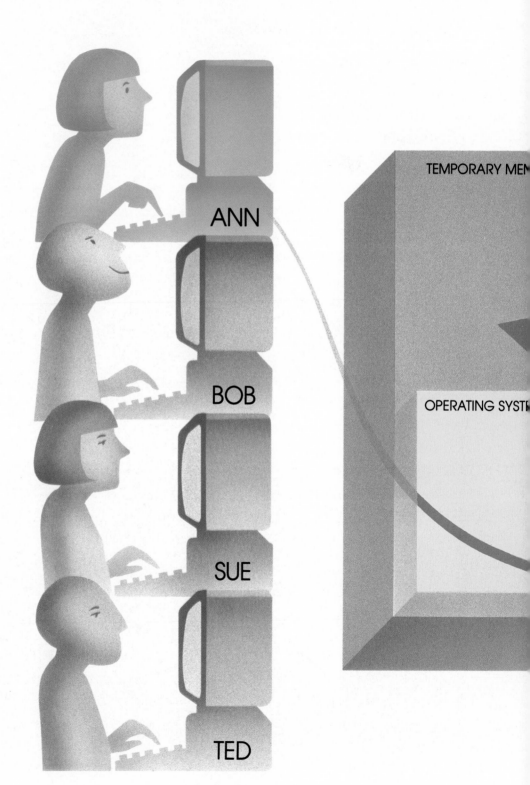

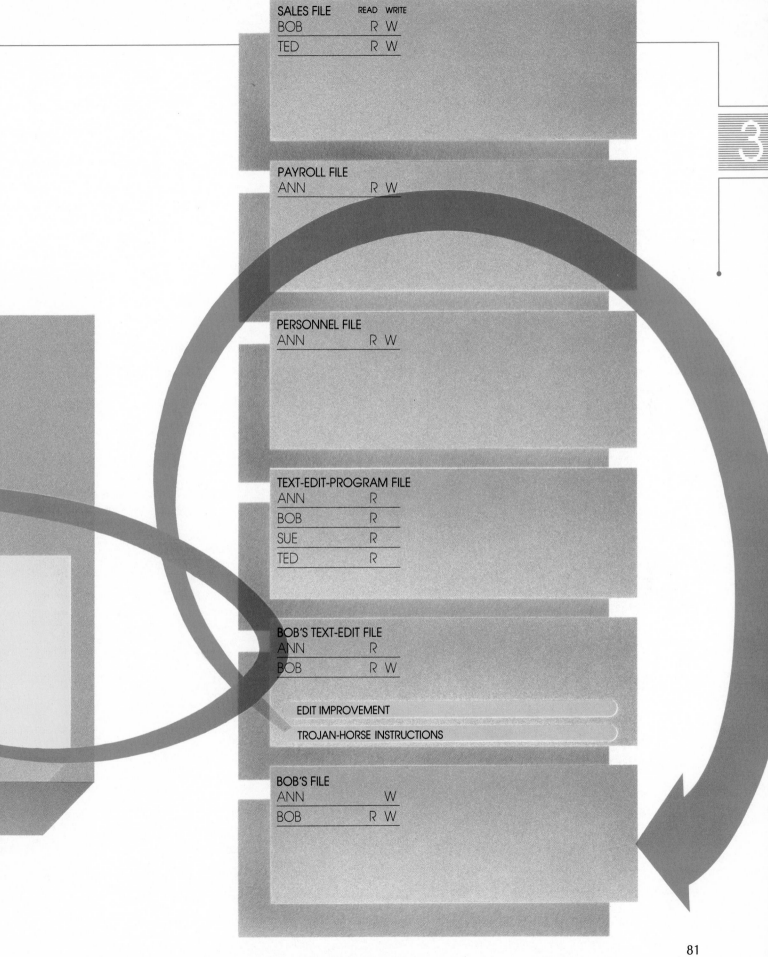

SALES FILE   READ   WRITE

	READ	WRITE
BOB	R	W
TED	R	W

PAYROLL FILE

ANN	R	W

PERSONNEL FILE

ANN	R	W

TEXT-EDIT-PROGRAM FILE

ANN	R
BOB	R
SUE	R
TED	R

BOB'S TEXT-EDIT FILE

ANN	R	
BOB	R	W

EDIT IMPROVEMENT

TROJAN-HORSE INSTRUCTIONS

BOB'S FILE

ANN		W
BOB	R	W

Erecting a Barrier against a Trojan Horse

One of the best defenses against a software Trojan horse is a set of operating-system programs known collectively as a reference monitor. A reference monitor defines each request for access as a reference to a specific file and, as shown on the following two pages, monitors all references by subjecting them to a strict protocol.

Reference monitors may be designed in a variety of ways, but each places a filter between users and stored computer files; the filter must be tamperproof but simple enough to allow system designers to test it easily. Generally, reference monitors work by assigning each file and each user a security classification. Files and users may be divided into only two categories, classified and unclassified, or they may be ranked in a hierarchy of security levels like that employed by governments to classify state secrets and military information.

In the system shown here, the reference monitor consists of a two-part filter. The first part contains two rules that apply to all users. According to Rule 1, users may read only those files at or below their own security classification; they may not see files classified at a higher level. Rule 2 forbids users to write into files below their own level, blocking any flow of classified information into less secure files. If a user's request for access to a file passes the tests in the first part of the filter, it is then tested against a file-user list to satisfy the second part; the list contains the names of all files and their authorized users, specifying read-access, write-access or both.

A reference monitor does have an Achilles' heel: The system does not foil a Trojan horse if the electronic burglar happens to have a security classification matching that of the file being stolen. However, because a reference-monitor system may employ numerous security levels, authorized users at a given classification may be few indeed—severely limiting the number of suspects in the event of a security breach.

The four users shown here and on the following two pages have been divided into two color-coded security levels: pink for access to classified files, purple for unclassified files. In practice, most reference-monitor systems would employ many more levels of security classification.

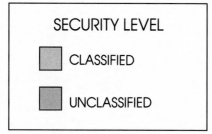

SECURITY LEVEL

CLASSIFIED

UNCLASSIFIED

REFERENCE MONITOR

SALES	READ	WRITE
BOB	R	W
TED	R	W

PAYROLL		
ANN	R	W

PERSONNEL		
ANN	R	W

TEXT-EDIT PROGRAM		
ANN	R	
BOB	R	
SUE	R	
TED	R	

BOB'S TEXT EDIT		
ANN	R	
BOB	R	W

BOB'S FILE		
ANN		W
BOB	R	W

1

Rule One:
Cannot read
a higher
classification

2

Rule Two:
Cannot write
to a lower
classification

SALES FILE	READ	WRITE
BOB	R	W
TED	R	W

PAYROLL FILE		
ANN	R	W

PERSONNEL FILE		
ANN	R	W

TEXT-EDIT-PROGRAM FILE		
ANN	R	
BOB	R	
SUE	R	
TED	R	

BOB'S TEXT-EDIT FILE		
ANN	R	
BOB	R	W

BOB'S FILE		
ANN		W
BOB	R	W

le requests must pass through a two-part
ter. The first part, consisting of two rules,
reens out requests to read higher-level
es *(Rule 1)* and blocks attempts to write into
wer-level files *(Rule 2)*. A request that sur-
ves the first part of the filter is then tested
ainst the file-user list in the second part.

Like the users in this example, files are also
divided into two color-coded security levels:
pink for classified, purple for unclassified.
None of the files is headed by an access-control
list; rather, all access-control information is
contained in the reference monitor.

Impenetrable Ciphers

Near Culpeper, Virginia, in the farming and horse-raising country southwest of Washington, D.C., stands an unimposing two-story building constructed of concrete block. A no-trespassing sign dissuades the casually curious from stepping beyond the decorative wood-rail fence that surrounds the structure, but visitors are not challenged until they reach the door. There, guards posted inside scrutinize them over closed-circuit television before granting admission.

Security is tight here because vast fortunes pass through the building each day. Yet the amount of cash on hand rarely exceeds the sum of whatever money the employees may have in their pockets and purses. The facility belongs to S.W.I.F.T., the Society for Worldwide Interbank Financial Telecommunications. Headquartered in Belgium, S.W.I.F.T. exists solely to provide electronic-funds-transfer (EFT) services to banks and other financial institutions. S.W.I.F.T. processes about 700,000 transactions daily for more than 1,800 banks in 46 countries, and all without the exchange of a single piece of paper—not a bank note, not a check, not a deposit or withdrawal slip.

These transactions take the form of computer-generated payment messages that are transmitted by means of a modem connected to each network terminal. A member bank in the United States, for example, may be instructed to credit the account of a corporation in Germany with so many million dollars and debit a company in Singapore for the same amount.

As long as the messages remain within S.W.I.F.T.'s operations centers, they are safe. But as soon as they are transmitted to race along telephone wires, they become vulnerable. Unless special measures are taken, a modern Dalton Gang armed with computer and modem could intercept the payment instructions, then modify them so that the funds would be deposited in the gang's account instead of in the rightful one. Or an international terrorist could introduce spurious messages designed to throw the world financial system into chaos.

Yet such scenarios are highly unlikely, largely because of the form in which S.W.I.F.T. and other international networks transfer assets electronically. Before transmission, the contents of each payment message are scrambled by a combination of special computer hardware and software so that even a supremely brilliant and dedicated cryptanalyst equipped with a powerful computer would require more than a lifetime to extract the meaning.

S.W.I.F.T.'s encryption system is designed to forestall the kind of surreptitious holdups that have made victims of computerized financial institutions since the middle of the 1970s. For example, an ingenious Japanese engineer, armed with a tape recorder and an oscilloscope, tapped into the telephone system at the Hokkaido Bank and intercepted messages coming from automatic teller machines (ATMs) to the bank's central computer. From these communications, he copied customer names and identification numbers onto magnetic identification cards and used the cards to withdraw from ATMs 1.33 million yen (about $6,500) that belonged to other people. Thanks primarily to encipherment, S.W.I.F.T.

Data traveling between computers is vulnerable to interception by eavesdroppers. Encryption renders their efforts fruitless by rearranging the data into a jumble that makes no sense to anyone who does not possess the secret key needed to decipher it.

fore, a code need not be unbreakable to be of use, but only so troublesome that its "work factor"—the length of time required to crack it—renders the encoded information worthless by the time it is recovered.

Cryptography remained for the most part a matter of pencil and paper until after World War I, when machines took over. Part mechanical, part electrical, these devices not only produced strong ciphers, but substantially increased the speed at which information could be encoded or decoded. One such machine, known as the Enigma, set the stage for the most celebrated code-breaking operation in history and led indirectly to the construction of the world's first large-scale digital machine.

The Enigma was invented in the early 1920s by a little-known German engineer, a Berliner named Arthur Scherbius. Intended for business use to keep confidential correspondence secret, Scherbius' device had a typewriter-like keyboard and electrical innards consisting of a maze of wires interconnecting three rotors that turned on a common shaft. The operator typed a letter of the plaintext to be encoded, and the rotors substituted a letter of ciphertext, or coded message, which lit up on a panel built into the machine. The operator then copied onto paper the letter that glowed and thus, a character at a time, encrypted the message. To decipher the message, the recipient needed an identical machine, along with a key to the initial rotor settings. Scherbius failed to convince the world of commerce that his machine merited their attention, and he died in obscurity.

But Scherbius' invention did not perish with him. When the German armies

began their sweep across Europe during the late 1930s, much of their radio traffic consisted of orders and other information encrypted on Arthur Scherbius' clever cipher device. However, Enigma's encoded messages did not fully satisfy the German high command. So the military improved the machine, adding a fourth and then a fifth rotor as well as other cipher-obscuring features. When it was finished, the Enigma was capable of scrambling a message in trillions of ways.

The British knew about Enigma, and in an attempt to master its workings, they established the code-breaking project known as *Ultra,* a name derived from the project's top-secret classification. This remarkable effort was centered at Bletchley Park, a Victorian mansion 47 miles north of London. Here, the government gathered the likes of the brilliant mathematician Alan Turing and Dillwyn Knox, a cryptanalyst who had cracked the German submarine code during World War I—while taking a bath, the story went. One writer has described the group as "a curious mixture of mathematicians, dons of various kinds, chess and crossword maestros, and an odd musician or two."

In penetrating the secrets of Enigma, Turing, Knox and their colleagues at Bletchley Park had an incalculable advantage. A replica of the machine and a description of how it worked had been smuggled out of Poland before that nation's fall in 1939. Thus forearmed, the British researchers were able to build electromechanical deciphering machines that, reversing the operation of the German device, scanned intercepted ciphertext until some linguistic pattern was discerned. Provided with such a clue, the cryptanalysts were well on the way to making sense of a message. The Germans made the job difficult by changing keys as often as three times a day. Yet Turing and Knox, by applying advanced methods of statistical analysis, were able to shorten radically the time needed by code breakers to puzzle out the keys to rotor settings. As a result, the master cryptanalysts at Bletchley Park often were able to decipher messages just hours after they had been sent. Midway through the war, the British began to intercept messages ciphered according to another system, which they code-named Fish. The Germans called it *Schlüsselzusatz*— coding attachment—and used it to circulate information and orders among the highest levels of command, including that of Hitler himself. The *Schlüsselzusatz,* with a complement of 12 rotors, was a far

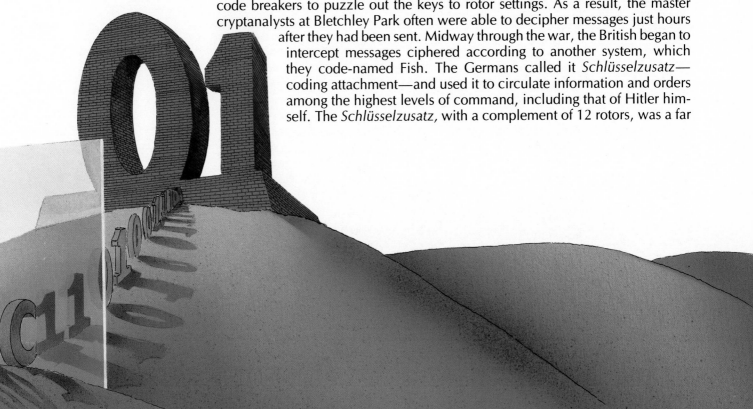

more complex machine than even late-model Enigmas, which could have as many as five rotors, and the new device produced ciphers that were correspondingly more difficult to penetrate.

The electromechanical devices at Bletchley Park, working with the speed of electric switches in a telephone exchange, operated much too slowly to break these improved ciphers. Responding to the new challenge in 1943, Turing prodded experimenters at the Post Office Research Station (the post office ran Britain's telephone systems) to build a faster, all-electronic code-breaking machine that would replace the plodding switches with lightning-fast vacuum tubes. Ultimately packed with 2,400 such tubes, this digital device predated the American ENIAC, the first large-scale computer, by two full years. Dubbed Colossus, the machine analyzed intercepted *Schlüsselzusatz* messages at the then-astonishing rate of 25,000 characters per second—fast enough to provide Allied battlefield commanders with timely foreknowledge of enemy intentions.

COMPUTER-AGE ENCRYPTION
By ushering in the age of electronic decryption techniques, Colossus marked a watershed in the history of cryptography. There could be only one defense against computers used to decipher messages: computers that could encipher them. Indeed, after the war, researchers began programming computers with encryption algorithms far more complex than those embodied in the rotors of an Enigma machine or a *Schlüsselzusatz*. The result was to increase the work factor to a level that more than matched the problem-solving potential of computers.

Like virtually all cryptography since Caesar's time, this new, computerized brand was kept under government wraps and employed almost exclusively to preserve military secrecy and guard diplomatic communications. But when time-sharing computer networks began to proliferate during the 1970s, they brought with them a widespread concern: that these networks, carriers of EFT messages and channels for proprietary information as well as confidential data about individuals, would be vulnerable to intruders and eavesdroppers. To foil them, mathematicians have formulated encryption schemes designed to protect electronic data in the private sector and in government agencies not charged with keeping official secrets.

Two encryption systems have led the way. One is a single-key system, in which data is both encrypted and decrypted with the same key, a sequence of eight numbers, each between zero and 127. The other is a two-key system; in this approach to cryptography, a pair of mathematically complementary keys, each containing as many as 200 digits, are used for encryption and decryption. In contrast with ciphers of earlier generations, where security depended in part on concealing the algorithm, confidentiality of a computer-encrypted message hinges solely on the secrecy of keys. Each system is thought to encrypt a message so inscrutably that the step-by-step mathematical algorithms can be made public without compromising security.

The single-key system, named the Data Encryption Standard (DES), was designated in 1977 as the official method for protecting unclassified computer data in agencies of the federal government. Its evolution began in 1973 when the U.S. National Bureau of Standards, responding to public concern about the confidentiality of computerized information outside military and diplomatic channels, invited the submission of data-encryption techniques as the first step toward an encryption scheme intended for public use.

The method selected by the bureau as the DES was developed by IBM researchers. During encryption, the DES algorithm divides a message into blocks of eight characters, then enciphers them one after another. Under control of the key, the letters and numbers of each block are scrambled no fewer than 16 times, resulting in eight characters of ciphertext *(pages 106-111)*.

AN INEXTRICABLE BOND

The DES links the enciphered blocks together in such a way that the encryption of each block, beginning with the second one, depends on the results of encoding the one that precedes it. Consequently, the final encrypted block is changed if a single character is altered anywhere in the message. This aspect of the DES is the basis for the Message Authentication Code, or MAC *(pages 110-111)*, which guarantees that any tampering with the contents of a message or with data filed away on disk or tape can be detected. The MAC can be used without encryption where the communications equipment in use cannot handle ciphertext and where it may be necessary to preserve the accuracy, though perhaps not the secrecy, of information passing between computers. For example, a bank may care little who finds out that it has transferred money from one account to another, but its reputation can be ruined if account numbers and transfer amounts are altered, whether accidentally or intentionally.

When cryptologists devise a new cipher such as the DES, others test it by trying to defeat it with two kinds of attack. One is known as the brute-force approach, an attempt to discover the key used to encrypt a message by systematically trying all possible keys. The other is an analytical attack, an effort to break the code by seeking out weaknesses in the algorithm that eliminate some of the possible keys from consideration.

Encompassing no fewer than 70 quadrillion possible keys, the DES appears secure against a brute-force attack. On average, an assailant would have to try half of them to find the one that unlocks the code. It has been estimated that this task would occupy even a speedy computer, able to generate one million trials per second, for 1,142 years. By then, the reason for making the attempt would have been long forgotten.

From an analytical standpoint, the DES appears equally sound. No cryptologist has found any alternative to trying all the keys one by one. Detractors point out that more than 200 of the DES's galaxy of keys are inferior ones. Called weak or semiweak or semi-semiweak keys by the experts, any of them might create clues in an encrypted message that could lead to its decipherment in less time than a brute-force attack would consume.

IBM and the Bureau of Standards caution against employing the weak keys. But Carl Meyer, one of the developers of the DES, denies that most of them offer an advantage to an attacker. "It is debatable how weak is weak," he says. "How you are going to attack the system is not clear. I would not hesitate to use a semi-semiweak key. I personally do not think you can do anything with them." Critics also note that the DES algorithm could have employed a key of 16 numbers, twice the present length. Such a key, they point out, would have substantially increased the DES's work factor.

The Case for Encrypting Computer Transmissions

Confidential computer data, unless encrypted, is never more vulnerable to theft than during transmission from one computer to another. In most cases, such information travels via the telephone system. In the short time required for data to travel from sender to receiver, the system affords eavesdroppers numerous opportunities to intercept the information and sometimes to alter it.

The uncertain journey begins at a modem attached to the transmitting computer. Plugged into the modem is a telephone line identical to the one leading from any standard telephone. In an office building *(left, below)*, this line is routed behind walls and between ceilings and floors to a small room called a telephone closet.

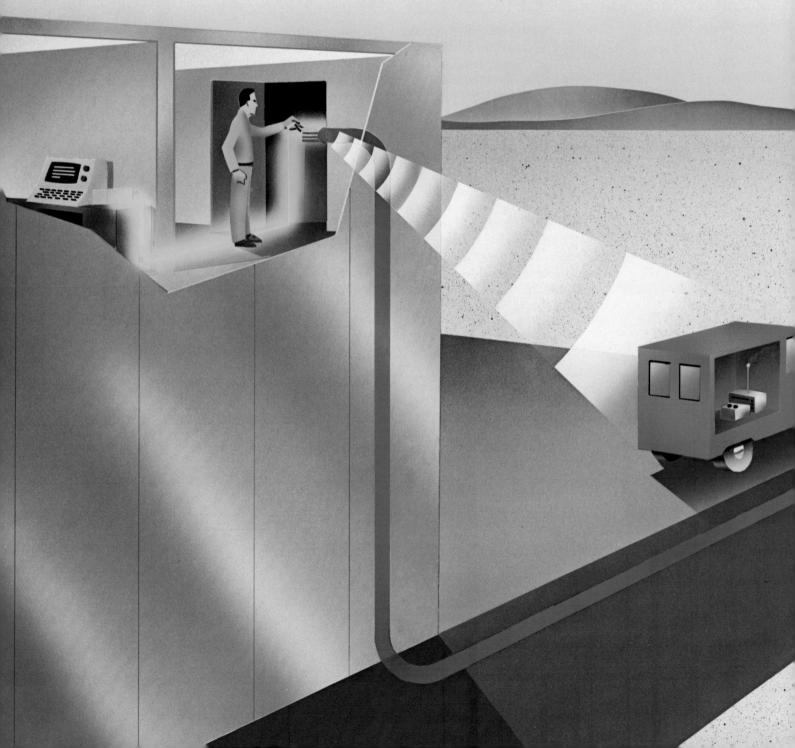

All the wires in a telephone closet are gathered into a cable, which is usually consolidated with others in the basement of the building. From there, a larger cable, about three inches in diameter, runs underground to a building called a central office, the headquarters for several exchanges (an exchange consists of local telephone numbers beginning with the same prefix). Here, data going to another computer on the exchange follows a similar path in reverse, directly to the receiving computer's modem. Information being transmitted to a modem on a different exchange is routed to the appropriate central office for connection. Between central offices, data may continue along its journey by cable, or it may be converted into a radio signal. Radio signals may be relayed to their destination by so-called repeater stations on the ground or by communications satellites. Eavesdropping is simplest and least expensive at either end of the transmission, near the source of the data or near its destination. Once individual telephone lines have been merged into cables, they are difficult to identify. Isolating a particular signal from a satellite transmission is even more challenging and costly. But because an eavesdropper can listen in on a transmission from a distance, intercepting computer data from space carries little risk of discovery (*page 96*).

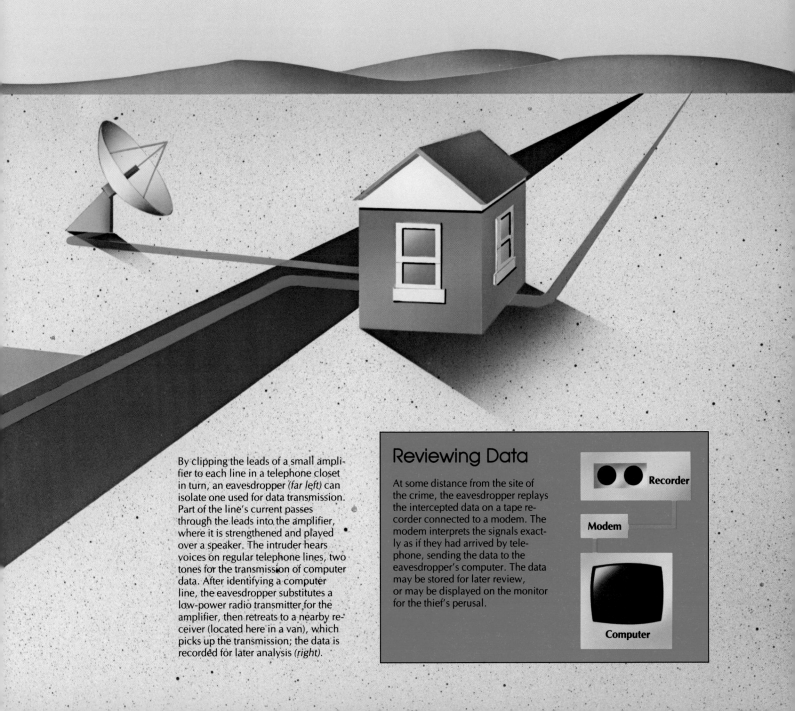

By clipping the leads of a small amplifier to each line in a telephone closet in turn, an eavesdropper *(far left)* can isolate one used for data transmission. Part of the line's current passes through the leads into the amplifier, where it is strengthened and played over a speaker. The intruder hears voices on regular telephone lines, two tones for the transmission of computer data. After identifying a computer line, the eavesdropper substitutes a low-power radio transmitter for the amplifier, then retreats to a nearby receiver (located here in a van), which picks up the transmission; the data is recorded for later analysis *(right)*.

Reviewing Data

At some distance from the site of the crime, the eavesdropper replays the intercepted data on a tape recorder connected to a modem. The modem interprets the signals exactly as if they had arrived by telephone, sending the data to the eavesdropper's computer. The data may be stored for later review, or may be displayed on the monitor for the thief's perusal.

Recorder

Modem

Computer

Snatching Data from the Ether

Computer data relayed to earth by a telephone-system communications satellite can be received from any location in an area covering millions of miles of the earth's surface. This broad coverage makes it quite easy for an eavesdropper to intercept computer data with a receiving system that employs an antenna similar to the satellite dishes commonly used with television sets.

Intercepting a communications satellite signal may be simple, but interpreting it is a daunting task. A satellite broadcasts on thousands of channels simultaneously, each representing one call, by means of an electronic process called multiplexing. The challenge for an eavesdropper is to discover which of the thousands of messages emanating from a satellite are of interest. Doing so demands an expert's knowledge of satellite communications as well as equipment costing several thousand dollars (right).

Intercepting data from space is accomplished most easily if the eavesdropper's target leases a satellite communications channel. Without the certainty that the information always is transmitted over the same route, an eavesdropper must monitor all channels continuously. Generally, this constant surveillance would require resources comparable with those of a national government or a multinational corporation.

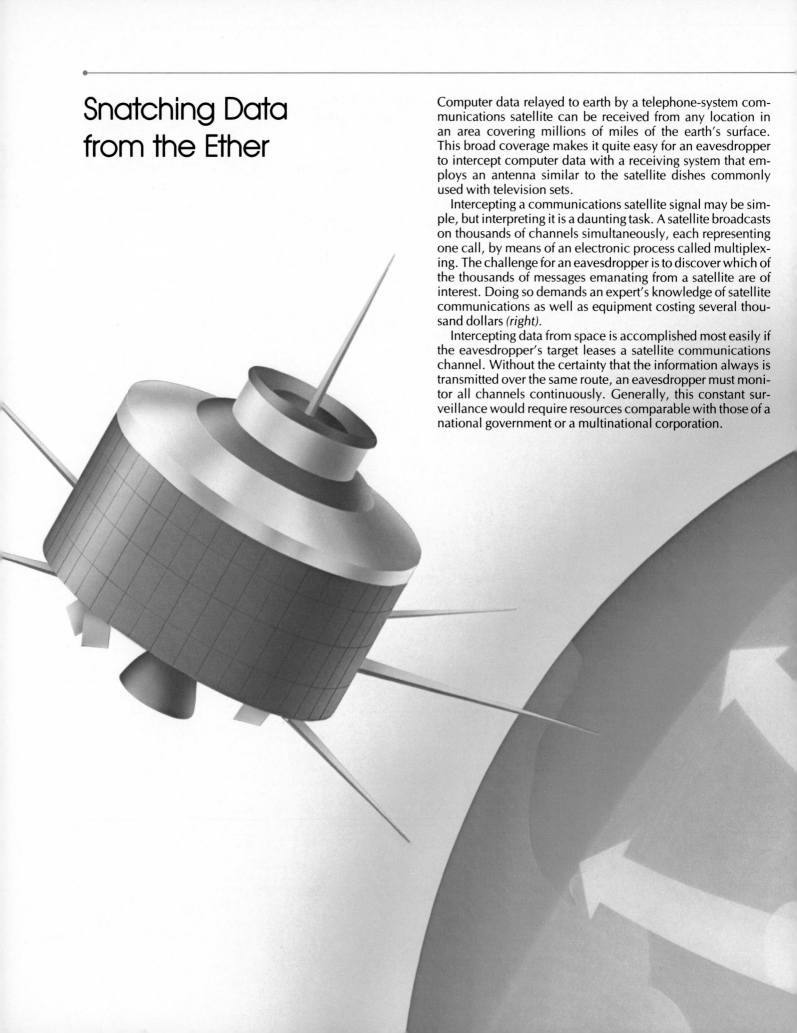

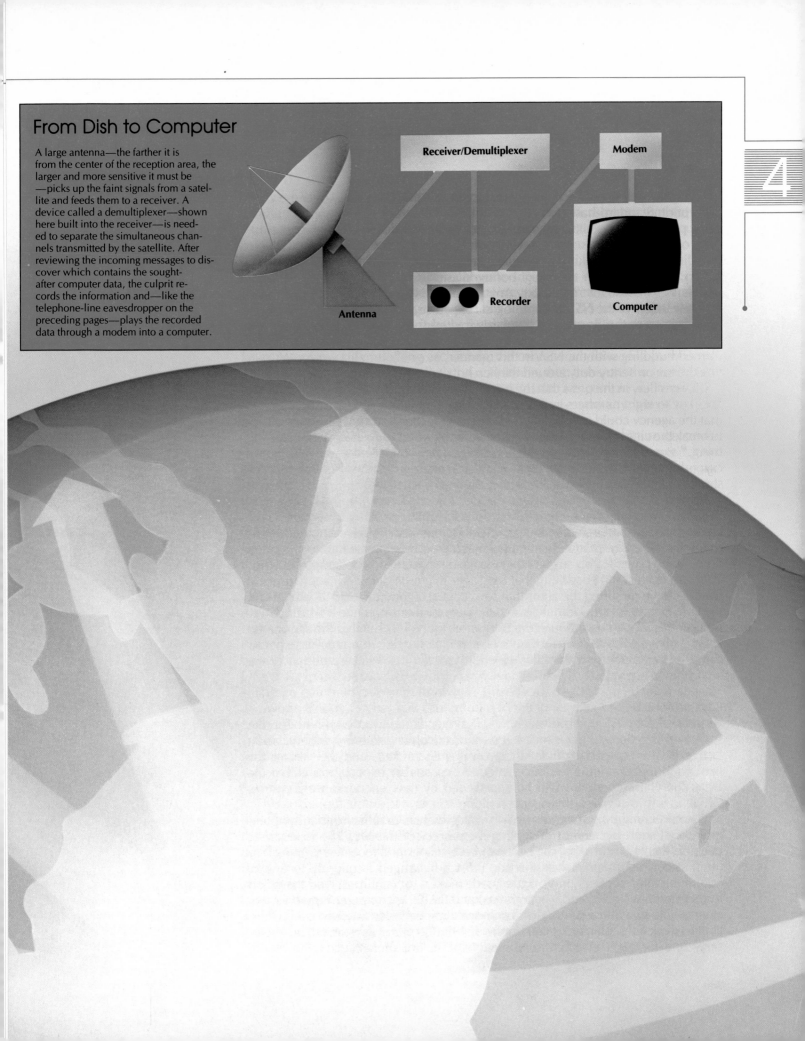

From Dish to Computer

A large antenna—the farther it is from the center of the reception area, the larger and more sensitive it must be—picks up the faint signals from a satellite and feeds them to a receiver. A device called a demultiplexer—shown here built into the receiver—is needed to separate the simultaneous channels transmitted by the satellite. After reviewing the incoming messages to discover which contains the sought-after computer data, the culprit records the information and—like the telephone-line eavesdropper on the preceding pages—plays the recorded data through a modem into a computer.

Receiver/Demultiplexer

Modem

Recorder

Computer

Antenna

Tools of Concealment

Encryption and decryption are two sides of the same coin: A message is made unintelligible by altering it according to a certain procedure; it is made intelligible again by applying a reverse procedure. The jumbling can be done at the level of whole words (replacing the word "attack" with a specified word such as "blue," for example) or at the level of individual letters and numerals. Encryption systems that operate at the word level are technically known as codes; those that work at the character level are called cipher systems. Both the DES and the public-key method belong to the latter group. In the language of cryptography, the original message is known as the plaintext, the disguised message as the ciphertext. Either the secret rules governing the method of encryption or the list of substitute words or letters (as in a code book, for instance) constitutes the key for encrypting and decrypting a message; sometimes both are required.

Five common techniques for scrambling a message are explained here; each encrypts the same message: SELL 100 SHARES OF ABCD INDUSTRIES. JOHN SMITH. As seen on the following pages, these treatments—substitution, blocking, permutation, expansion and compaction—are actually used repeatedly and in combination with one another during the ciphering of a message by the DES. (Throughout these examples, a dot symbol represents a space.)

SUBSTITUTION

The first step in this process is to create a substitution table *(right)*, designating the replacement character for each character (including spaces and punctuation marks) that might appear in the message. Here, J is specified as the substitute for any A in the message, 2 for any F, and so on. The next line shows the ciphertext formed when the table is applied to the plaintext—SELL 100 SHARES OF ABCD INDUSTRIES. JOHN SMITH.—turning the first letter, S, into the numeral 5, for example. Below the ciphertext is the key, the reverse of the substitution table. Here, the substitute characters appear in conventional alphabetic and numeric order. Applying the table reveals the plaintext.

A	B	C	D	E	F	G	H	I	J	K	L	M	N	O	P	Q	R	S	T	U	V	W	X	Y	Z	1	2	3	4	5	6	7	8	9	0	·	,	.
J	U	T	K	P	2	N	4	B	Q	·	E	3	C	,	7	D	Y	5	R	9	·	G	6	A	O	I	F	0	8	H	S	M	W	L	V	X	Z	1

Replacement Characters

5 P E E X I V V X 5 4 J Y P 5 X , 2 X J U T K X B C K 9 5 R Y B P 5 1 X Q , 4 C X 5 3 B R 4 1

Encrypted Message

A	B	C	D	E	F	G	H	I	J	K	L	M	N	O	P	Q	R	S	T	U	V	W	X	Y	Z	1	2	3	4	5	6	7	8	9	0	·	,	.
Y	I	N	Q	L	2	W	5	1	A	D	9	7	G	Z	E	J	T	6	C	B	0	8	·	R	,	.	F	M	H	S	X	P	4	U	3	K	O	V

Replacement Characters

S E L L · 1 0 0 · S H A R E S · O F · A B C D · I N D U S T R I E S . · J O H N · S M I T H .

Decrypted Message

BLOCKING

Encryption systems often divide a message into blocks of characters that are independently manipulated. In the example here, the message was blocked into groups of eight characters and symbols (including a dot for each space). The resulting six blocks were then realigned vertically, with an extra space inserted into the sixth vertical block to make it even with the others. The ciphertext is created by blocking the new stack horizontally—to yield eight groups of six characters each—and transmitting these blocks in sequence. The receiver will group the ciphertext into blocks of six characters, stack them and read the message in the vertical columns.

S	·	O	I	E	·	BLOCK 1
E	S	F	N	S	S	BLOCK 2
L	H	·	D	.	M	BLOCK 3
L	A	A	U	·	I	BLOCK 4
·	R	B	S	J	T	BLOCK 5
1	E	C	T	O	H	BLOCK 6
O	S	D	R	H	.	BLOCK 7
O	·	·	I	N	·	BLOCK 8

Vertical Alignment

BLOCK 1	BLOCK 2	BLOCK 3	BLOCK 4	BLOCK 5	BLOCK 6	BLOCK 7	BLOCK 8
S · O I E ·	E S F N S S	L H · D . M	L A A U · I	· R B S J T	1 E C T O H	O S D R H .	O · · I N ·

Realigned Message

PERMUTATION

One of the most important encryption techniques is permutation, also called transposition. It involves moving characters around according to specific rules; the characters keep their identity but not their position—the opposite of substitution, in which characters keep their position but change their identity. In the example at right, the first step is to block the message into groups of eight. Then, in each group, the first and last characters are transposed, as are the middle two characters. The receiver subjects the ciphertext to exactly the same treatment in order to read the message.

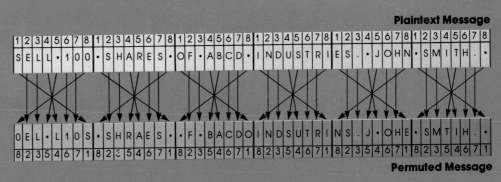

Plaintext Message

Permuted Message

EXPANSION

A simple way to obscure a message is to stretch it according to a fixed recipe. Here, the expansion follows the rules of the children's coding system called Pig Latin. Each word is altered by putting the first consonant sound last and adding the suffix "ay," as in "oybay" for "boy." (If a word begins with a vowel, the suffix "way" is

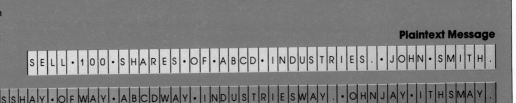

Plaintext Message

Expanded Message

simply added.) In actual cryptographic practice, the recipe would be much more elaborate. Moreover, expansion is often combined with other encryption techniques, since a cipher based on stretching alone is easily broken.

COMPACTION

Reducing the length of a message or the number of its blocks is another way of rendering the message unreadable. The formula for compaction in the elementary example shown here is to remove every third character, punctuation mark or space. The components that have been removed are transmitted separately to the message receiver *(bottom row).* That person knows the rule used for removal of the components and therefore knows where to reinsert them so that the message can be restored to its original form. The combination of the removed letters and the rule for removing them makes up the key for decrypting the message.

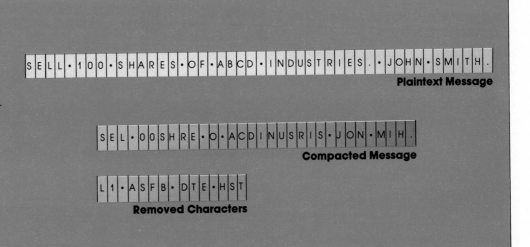

Plaintext Message

Compacted Message

Removed Characters

SEND MESSAGE, ENCRYPT WITH DATA ENCRYPTION STANDARD

ENTER YOUR KEY

81 56 3 33 127 72 125 94

TO:

JULIA EDWARDS

TEXT:

SELL 100 SHARES OF ABCD INDUSTRIES. JOHN SMITH.

In this example of transmitting a message by the DES, the sender types an initial instruction to select the method of encryption, then responds to prompts by the computer.

An Overview of the DES

As suggested by the pair of monitor screens on these pages, computers do virtually all of the work in encrypted communications. The sender and receiver of a message never have to see it in its ciphered form. When using the DES, for example, the sender merely activates the program, then enters the secret key and the message; to read the message, the receiver activates the same program and enters the same key. The message appears on the screen with no indication of the millions of arithmetical operations that sealed the information from prying eyes.

Encryption by the DES is usually done using a microchip and other hardware specially designed for the job. The sophisticated multistep routine, or algorithm, built into the chip includes the encryption tactics of substitution, blocking, per-

The Route to Encryption

The DES method starts by dividing a message into blocks of eight characters. Blocks are encrypted individually.

Each block is translated into bits, which are then rearranged according to a formula.

The new permutation of bits is split into a right-side block and a left-side block.

The right-side block is expanded according to a formula before going on to join the key.

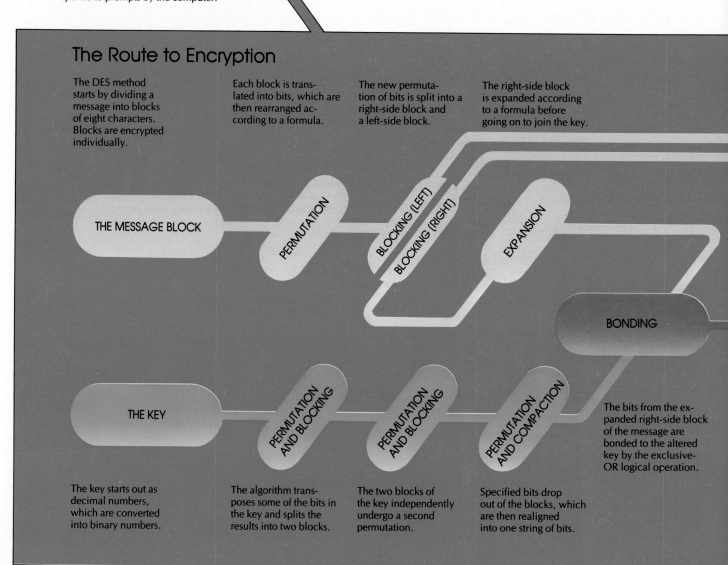

THE MESSAGE BLOCK

PERMUTATION

BLOCKING (LEFT)

BLOCKING (RIGHT)

EXPANSION

BONDING

THE KEY

PERMUTATION AND BLOCKING

PERMUTATION AND BLOCKING

PERMUTATION AND COMPACTION

The bits from the expanded right-side block of the message are bonded to the altered key by the exclusive-OR logical operation.

The key starts out as decimal numbers, which are converted into binary numbers.

The algorithm transposes some of the bits in the key and splits the results into two blocks.

The two blocks of the key independently undergo a second permutation.

Specified bits drop out of the blocks, which are then realigned into one string of bits.

mutation, expansion and compaction. An additional procedure—a logical operation called exclusive-OR *(box, below)*—is used to bond components of the cipher at various points along the way. Although the algorithm is fixed, a given message or piece of data can be encrypted in 70 quadrillion different ways—the number of possible secret keys the system will allow. Clearly, then, key management—the ensuring of key secrecy—is a principal factor in guaranteeing the security of the message or data.

Below is a flow chart of the basic process (a more detailed explanation appears on pages 108-111). The first step in the encryption chain is to divide the message into blocks. Each block is then individually subjected to the steps indicated in the chart. But that is just the beginning: Before the block is completely encrypted, it must cycle through 15 additional rounds of the process; each round will impose the same sequence of steps shown in the chart.

CHECK MESSAGES

JOHN SMITH OCTOBER 25 10:10 AM

READ MESSAGE, DECRYPT WITH DATA ENCRYPTION STANDARD

ENTER YOUR KEY

81 56 3 33 127 72 125 94

SELL 100 SHARES OF ABCD INDUSTRIES. JOHN SMITH. 8V•?

The receiver checks her electronic mail and engages in a dialogue with the computer to read the message. The last three characters and a space verify an accurate transmission.

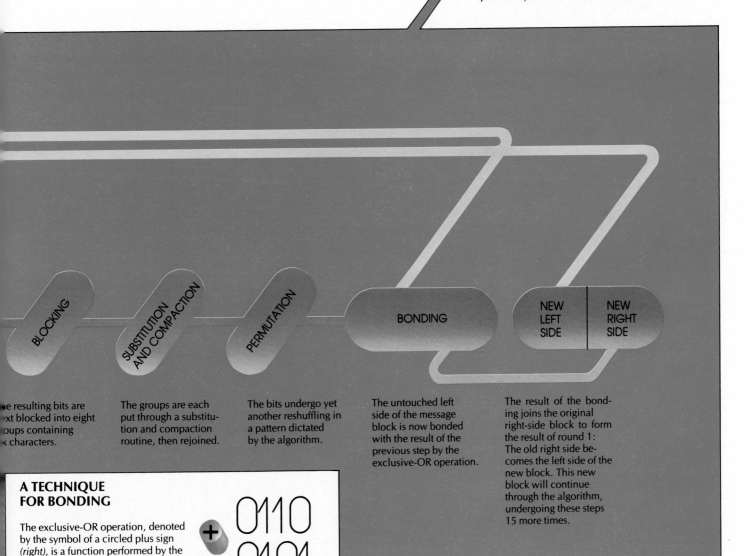

BLOCKING

SUBSTITUTION AND COMPACTION

PERMUTATION

BONDING

NEW LEFT SIDE

NEW RIGHT SIDE

...e resulting bits are ...xt blocked into eight ...oups containing ... characters.

The groups are each put through a substitution and compaction routine, then rejoined.

The bits undergo yet another reshuffling in a pattern dictated by the algorithm.

The untouched left side of the message block is now bonded with the result of the previous step by the exclusive-OR operation.

The result of the bonding joins the original right-side block to form the result of round 1: The old right side becomes the left side of the new block. This new block will continue through the algorithm, undergoing these steps 15 more times.

A TECHNIQUE FOR BONDING

The exclusive-OR operation, denoted by the symbol of a circled plus sign *(right)*, is a function performed by the logic gates in a computer's circuitry. Its rules are simple: When unlike bits (zero and one) are combined, the result is a one; when similar bits (two ones or two zeros) are combined, the result is a zero.

$$\oplus \quad \begin{array}{c} 0110 \\ 0101 \\ \hline 0011 \end{array}$$

A Close-Up of the DES

All of the jumbling wrought by the DES algorithm takes place in the computer's language of bits—the binary digits zero and one. The key and the message are translated into binary by different means. Initially, the key is made up of eight decimal numbers; these are simply turned into their seven-bit binary equivalents, with an extra bit added at the end for checking. The DES algorithm uses only the first seven bits for encryption, however; the checking bit is ignored. Thus, when put into action by the DES, a key is eight decimal numbers times seven bits, or 56 bits long.

The message is converted to binary by expressing it in ASCII—the American Standard Code for Information Interchange. ASCII, shown in abbreviated form on pages 120-121, is an agreed-upon list of binary representations of the roman alphabet, the numbers of the decimal system, punctuation marks and other keyboard symbols. ASCII codes are eight bits in length—seven plus a leading checking bit. Because the message is encrypted in blocks of eight characters, each block starts out as 64 bits *(opposite, top)*.

Provided the key remains secret, its 56-bit length is a formi-dable defense against an attack on the ciphertext. A would-be code breaker using a computer to test all possible combinations of 56 zeros and ones at the rate of one million tests a second could expect to take 1,142 years to complete the task.

An additional safeguard is the sheer complexity of the algorithm. As indicated by the flow chart on the preceding pages, the 64 bits of each block of the message are permuted and divided into two sides that proceed separately through the algorithm to form the starting point for the next round of encryption. Each block must pass through 16 rounds of garbling, with the key jumbled into a new form, or subkey, for each round. Each subkey is derived from the one preceding it, and each is bonded with a piece of the message by the exclusive-OR operation, so that the message is thoroughly imbued with the key's uniqueness.

A detailed example of the DES in action is traced on these two pages. Under the control of a randomly generated key *(below)*, the first of the 16 rounds of ciphering is done on the initial eight-unit block of the message SELL 100 SHARES OF ABCD INDUSTRIES. JOHN SMITH.

The Creation of Keys

The key shared by sender and receiver consists of eight decimal numbers, each between 0 and 127. Typically, a key is generated by computer to ensure that the numbers are random—lacking a detectable pattern. In this example, the numbers making up the key are 81, 56, 3, 33, 127, 72, 125 and 94. The computer converts them to their binary equivalents, with leading zeros to fill out the seven digits required by the algorithm and an eighth bit for checking. The bits are then grouped into blocks, the checking bit is ignored, and the bits are subjected to permutation and compaction. The process is repeated 15 times to produce unique subkeys for each subsequent round.

Each bit in the binary equivalent for each decimal number *(top)* is given a position number *(bottom)*.

The bits are resequenced (old position numbers are on top), and two 28-digit blocks are formed.

In each block, bits are shifted one place to the left (the first goes to the end). In subsequent rounds, the bits may shift more places.

Bits are dropped and the 48-bit result is subkey 1. New subkeys are made by going back a step, doing another left shift and repeating this step.

Message Block's Progress

message is blocked
groups of eight charac-
, spaces and punctua-
marks. The computer
slates each of the eight
ponents into ASCII,
ducing 64 bits in all.
e—as with the key—
h bit has a position
mber shown below it.

bits are resequenced.
bit that was in position
shifted to position 1;
bit that was in position
goes to position 2; and
on. The string is split
two 32-bit blocks: left
e and right side.

right side is expanded
8 bits by repeating
tain bits, such as those
e in positions 4 and 5.
exclusive-OR operation
one with subkey 1.

result is blocked into
-bit groups. Each group
dergoes substitution and
paction. The results are
ed into a 32-bit string.
, in turn, is subjected to
escribed resequencing.

left-side block, un-
ched until now, is
ught in and aligned with
result of the previous
, and an exclusive-OR
eration is performed.

ULT OF ROUND 1
result becomes the
t side for round 2. The
ginal, unaltered right
e becomes the left side.

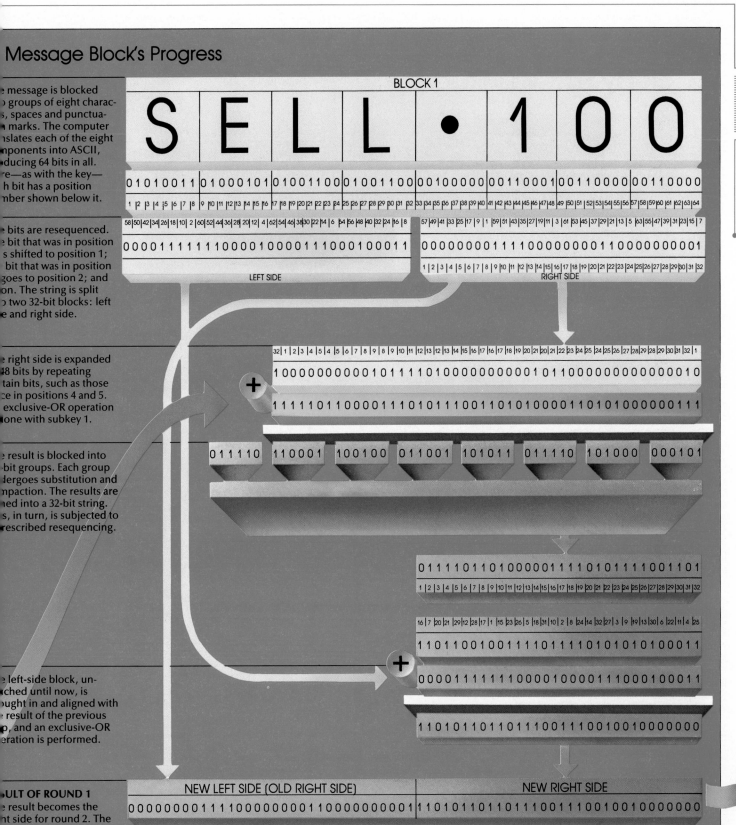

A Round-by-Round, Block-by-Block Linkage

At the end of round 1, the first block of the message has scarcely begun its ordeal; 15 more rounds are required before the DES algorithm moves on to encrypt the next block. For each message block, the same subkeys are used at identical stages of encryption—subkey 1 for round 1, subkey 2 for round 2 and so on.

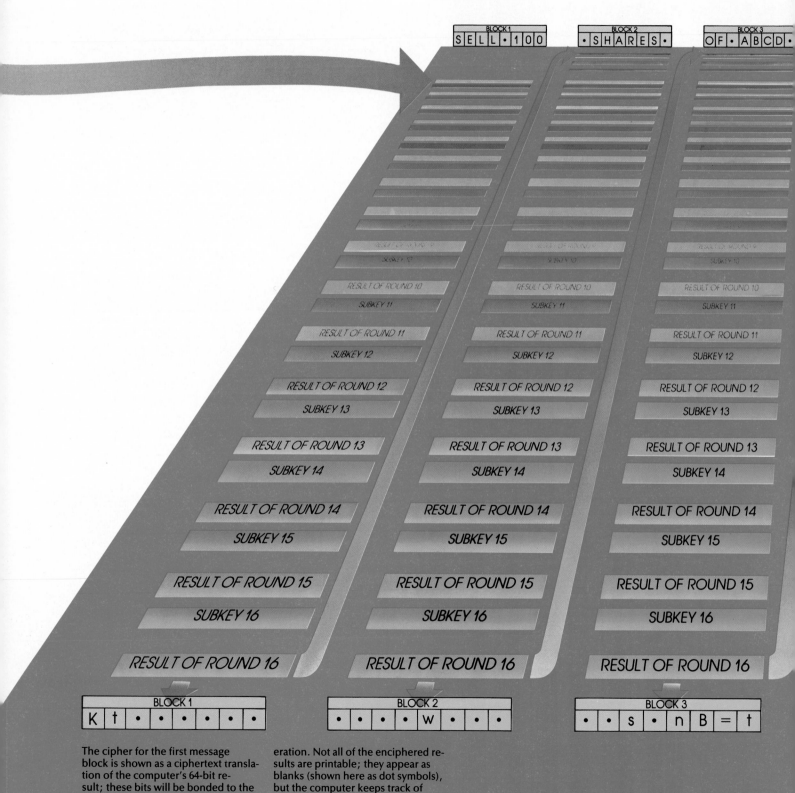

The cipher for the first message block is shown as a ciphertext translation of the computer's 64-bit result; these bits will be bonded to the next block by an exclusive-OR operation. Not all of the enciphered results are printable; they appear as blanks (shown here as dot symbols), but the computer keeps track of their ciphered meaning.

A block-linking stratagem adds to the defensive strength of the encrypted message: The cipher of each message block is bonded to the next block by an exclusive-OR operation, so that every step of the encryption process shapes every subsequent step. The last block of an encrypted message (or a portion of the block) can thus act as a Message Authentication Code (MAC). Sent separately from the ciphered message, the MAC is used to check the accuracy of the transmission: The receiver reencrypts the message; if the encrypted last block differs from the MAC, it means the message was altered en route. (A sender may also append a MAC to the end of a plaintext message as a check against alteration.)

The first 32 bits—four units—of the last block are often picked as the MAC. The receiver recomputes the message and looks for a match.

The Power of Two Keys

SEND MESSAGE, ENCRYPT WITH PUBLIC
KEY

TO:

JULIA EDWARDS

TEXT:

SELL 100 SHARES OF ABCD INDUSTRIES.
JOHN SMITH.

For all its virtues, the Data Encryption Standard has its flaws. To begin with, ensuring the secure distribution of secret keys between each pair of senders and receivers is difficult, especially when the network of users is large. A 1,000-person network, for example, would require almost half a million keys to guarantee the privacy of each pair. More important, the MAC feature, though it acts as a check on the information transmitted, does not prevent a person from sending himself a message (to order a transfer of funds, for instance).

The public-key system of encryption addresses both of these problems. For a network of 1,000 persons only 2,000 keys are needed. Each user has a pair of mathematically related keys: One is public knowledge within the network, the other is known only to its owner. The sender encrypts a message using the receiver's public key; the receiver decrypts it with the mathematically related private key. The sender's keys come into play to create and then to decrypt a

In this example, as with the DES, users of the public-key system respond to a series of computer prompts and observe none of the ciphering process. Here, sender John Smith activates the program and identifies the addressee, Julia Edwards. Behind the scenes, the computer retrieves Julia Edwards' public key and employs it to encrypt John Smith's message.

ASSIGNING NUMERIC VALUES

ENCRYPTIO

Converting a Message to Numbers

PRESCRIBED NUMERIC VALUES

A	B	C	D	E	F	G	H	I	J	K	L	M	N	O	P	Q	R	S	T	U	V	W	X	Y	Z	0	1	2	3	4	5	6	7	8	9	•	,	.
1	2	3	4	5	6	7	8	9	10	11	12	13	14	15	16	17	18	19	20	21	22	23	24	25	26	27	28	29	30	31	32	33	34	35	36	37	38	39

CONVERTING THE MESSAGE

S	E	L	L	•	1	0	0	•	S	H	A	R	E	S	•	O	F	•	A	B	C	D	•	I	N	D	U	S	T	R	I	E	S		•	J	O	H	N	•	S	M	I	T	H	•
19	5	12	12	37	28	27	27	37	19	8	1	18	5	19	37	15	6	37	1	2	3	4	37	9	14	4	21	19	20	18	9	5	19	37	37	10	15	8	14	37	19	13	9	20	8	39

Before a message can be encrypted by the public-key method, it must be blocked and each block assigned a numerical value. Blocks may vary in size, from one character to several; and numerical values may be assigned in many ways, within constraints imposed by the system. In the example used here, each character is treated as a block, and a simple number-assigning system is used: A = 1, B = 2, C = 3, D = 4, and so on (table at top).

When John Smith types the message into his computer, every character, space and punctuation mark is assigned its specified numerical value (table, above). These numbers will be individually subjected to a series of arithmetical operations controlled by both the public key and the private key.

N = 137707713508583179288209998059680673614385798795679982806039889920592617865629107951789097723014337685422634773542516590520660011

special signature that is used to verify the source of the message *(pages 116-117)*.

The strength of the public-key system depends on the nature of the relationship between the public and private keys; given a public key, it is virtually impossible to derive the private one. The system described here and on the following pages—designed by Ronald Rivest, Adi Shamir and Leonard Adleman while at M.I.T.—creates the keys by first multiplying two prime numbers (numbers evenly divisible only by themselves and one). Figuring out the primes from the product of the multiplication—a process called factoring—is exceedingly difficult. Small numbers are used here for clarity, but the algorithm actually works with very large numbers; on the bottom of these pages, for instance, is a 203-digit product of two primes. Factoring such a number would be the first step in trying to break a key; with present methods, it would take a computer millions of years.

CHECK MESSAGES

JOHN SMITH OCTOBER 25 10:10 AM

READ MESSAGE, DECRYPT WITH PUBLIC KEY

ENTER KEY FILE NAME

JEFILE

SELL 100 SHARES OF ABCD INDUSTRIES. JOHN SMITH.

ND DECRYPTION

SIGNING AND SEALING

On the receiving end, Julia Edwards periodically checks her computer for messages. When the computer indicates that one has arrived, she specifies that it be decrypted by the public-key method. She enters the name of the protected computer file that contains her private key: Jefile. Decryption proceeds invisibly, and the message then appears on the screen.

Creating Julia Edwards' Keys

1. Each user has a public and a private key, and each key has two parts. To create Julia Edwards' keys, two prime numbers, customarily designated P and Q, are generated by an operator at a central computer. (To qualify, a prime number must pass a special mathematical test.) Here, P is 7, Q is 17.

2. In this simplified example, the two primes are multiplied, and the result—N—will be the first part of both keys. Here, N is 119.

3. Next, an odd number is chosen, in this case, 5. (This number—designated E—must also pass a special mathematical test.) It forms the second part of the public key.

4. To create the second part of the private key, the numbers are multiplied: P minus 1 (6, in this case) times Q minus 1 (16) times E minus 1 (4). The result is 384.

5. Next, 1 is added to the result of the previous step, yielding 385.

6. The sum is divided by E (5). The result of the division, 77 (designated D), is the second part of Julia Edwards' private key.

1 $P = 7, Q = 17$

2 $7 \times 17 = 119 = N$

3 $E = 5$

4 $6 \times 16 \times 4 = 384$

5 $384 + 1 = 385$

6 $385 \div 5 = 77 = D$

PUBLIC KEY

119 5

PRIVATE KEY

119 77

At the end of the procedure Julia Edwards has a public key (119 5) and a private key (119 77). In reality, these numbers would be many digits long; as indicated on the screen above, she would keep the private key in a protected computer file.

562436680969616059933915069214871116068945792874446848974030485679 0943

The Public-Key System in Action

Once a message has been committed to public-key encryption, it is virtually beyond retrieval. Even if the sender wanted to pry apart the ciphertext for some reason, it would be a hopeless task. The cipher can be unscrambled only by the person who possesses the private key corresponding to the public key that was used for encrypting the message—that is, the addressee. Thus, any user with access to the network's directory of public keys may send anyone else a confidential

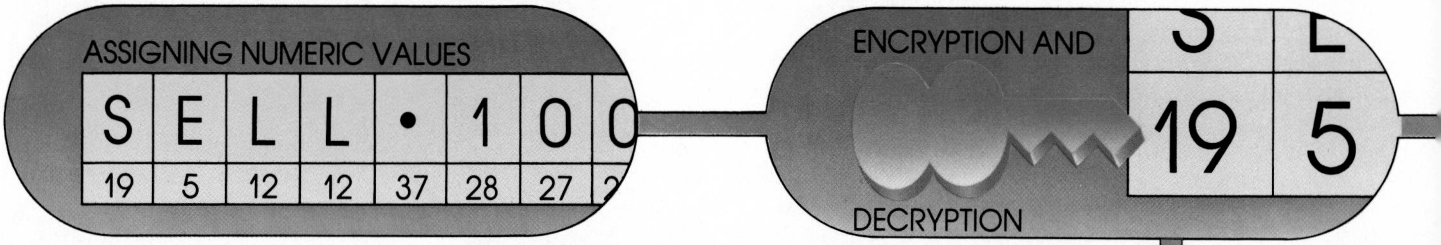

The Arithmetic of Locking and Unlocking

The number 19, assigned to the letter S, is raised to the fifth power (multiplied by itself five times), as dictated by the second part of Julia Edwards' public key (5).

The result of 19 raised to the fifth power—2,476,099—is divided by the first part of Julia Edwards' public key, the number 119.

The division yields the number 20,807 and a remainder of 66. Only the remainder is important: It is the value of the encrypted letter S.

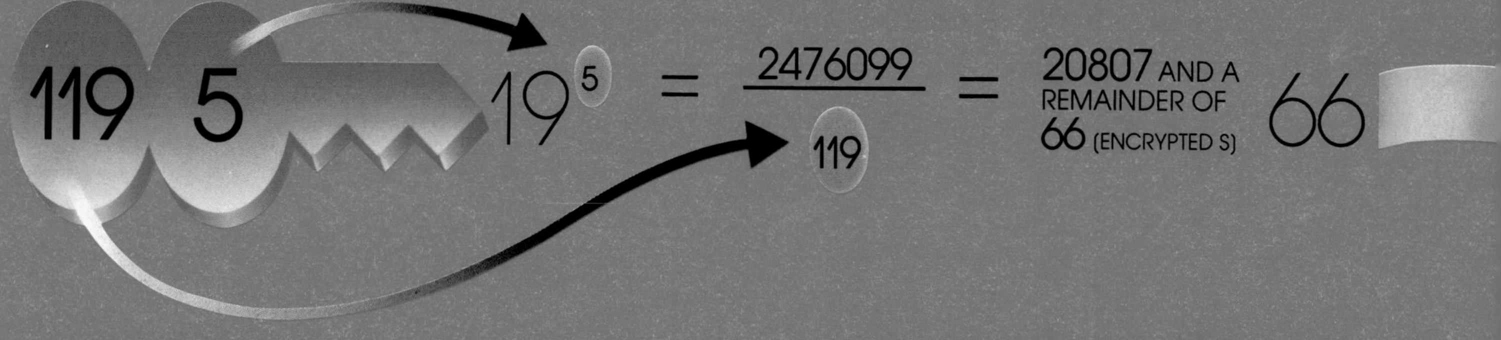

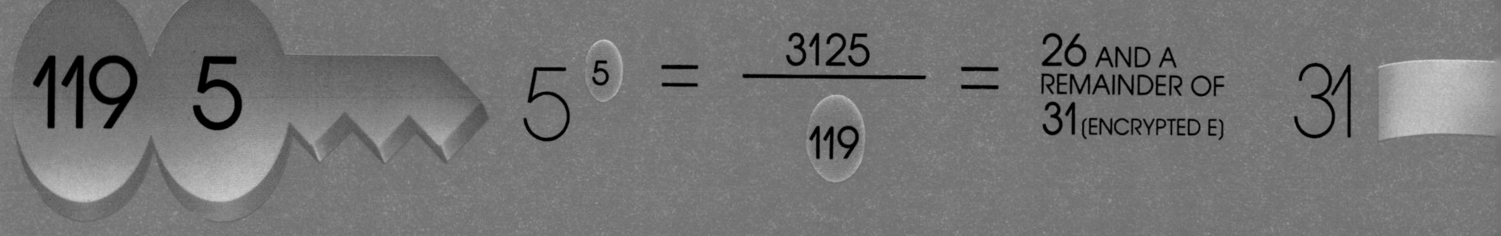

The next letter of the message, E, has the assigned value 5. Using the second part of the public key, this number is raised to the fifth power.

The result of multiplying 5 by itself five times—3,125—is divided by the other part of the public key, 119.

The division yields the number 26 and a remainder of 31. Again, only the remainder is significant. It is the value of the encrypted letter E.

message; but only the intended recipient can decipher it.

The process of ciphering and deciphering is shown below, using the artificially small numbers that make up Julia Edwards' keys and working on the first two letters of the message SELL 100 SHARES OF ABCD INDUSTRIES. JOHN SMITH. Unlike the DES—which manipulates the bits assigned to each component of the message through such techniques as substitution and compaction—the public-key system employs a purely mathematical process. In order to encrypt the message, the two numbers that make up the receiver's public key are used to perform computations on the numerical value assigned to every character, space and punctuation mark. Because the numbers in the public key have an inverse relationship with the numbers in the private key, the message may be decrypted by performing similar computations with the private-key numbers.

SIGNING AND SEALING

Decryption, using Julia Edwards' private key, follows the same steps. First, 66—the encrypted S—is raised to the 77th power, as dictated by the second part of the key.

The result of the previous step is divided by 119, the first part of Julia Edwards' private key, which is identical to the first part of her public key.

The remainder resulting from the division is 19—the original number assigned to the letter S. Thus, the decryption of the first one-letter block of the message is complete.

$$119 \quad 77 \quad 66^{77} = \frac{1273\ldots}{119} = 1069\ldots \text{ AND A REMAINDER OF } 19 \text{ (NUMERICAL EQUIVALENT OF) } S$$

$$119 \quad 77 \quad 31^{77} = \frac{6836\ldots}{119} = 5745\ldots \text{ AND A REMAINDER OF } 5 \text{ (NUMERICAL EQUIVALENT OF) } E$$

The number 31—the encrypted letter E—is raised to the 77th power, as dictated by the second part of Julia Edwards' private key.

The result of multiplying 31 by itself 77 times is divided by 119, the other part of the private key.

The remainder resulting from the division is 5—the original value assigned to the letter E. Each letter block will be decrypted in the same way.

A Twice-Scrambled Certificate of Origin

One of the chief attributes of the public-key system is its ability to verify the identity of the source of a message. This is made possible by a simple variation on the encryption techniques described on the preceding pages. Precisely how it is done depends on whether or not secrecy is important.

If the contents of a message are not secret but the receiver must be certain of the sender's identity, the message may be signed—that is, transmitted as a so-called digital signature. A signature is exceedingly difficult to counterfeit, because the message is encrypted not with the receiver's public key but

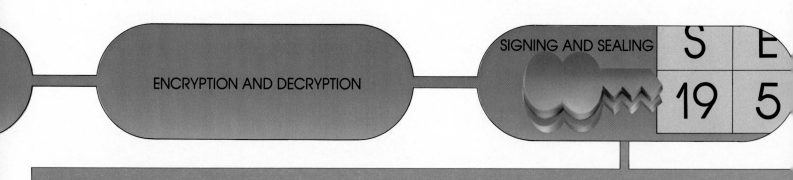

SIGNING AND SEALING

S	E
19	5

ENCRYPTION AND DECRYPTION

Two Tiers of Decryption

To begin the encryption technique called signing, the value of the letter S (19)—is raised to the 27th power, as dictated by the second part of John Smith's private key.

The result of raising 19 to the 27th power is divided by 55, the first part of his private key.

The division yields a very large number, which is disregarded, and a remainder of 24. This completes the signing process for the letter S; only John Smith's public key can decrypt it.

$$55 \quad 27 \qquad 19^{27} = \frac{3360....}{55} = 6109.... \text{ AND A REMAINDER OF } 24 \text{ (ENCRYPTED S)} \qquad 24$$

$$119 \quad 5 \qquad 24^{5} = \frac{7962624}{119} = 66912 \text{ AND A REMAINDER OF } 96 \text{ (DOUBLE-ENCRYPTED S)} \qquad 96$$

To seal the message for secrecy, the result of the first encryption, 24 in this case, is raised to the fifth power, as dictated by the second part of receiver Julia Edwards' public key.

The result of raising 24 to the fifth power is divided by 119, the other part of Julia Edwards' public key.

The division yields a number (disregarded) and a remainder of 96—the twice-encrypted S. It will be sent when the rest of the message has undergone the same double encryption.

with the sender's private key. Anyone who knew that the incoming message was sent by John Smith, for example, could decrypt it using John Smith's public key. But a forgery—a message encrypted with a different private key and transmitted as coming from John Smith—would produce only gibberish when the real John Smith's public key was applied to decrypt it. (A nonsecret message could also be transmitted as plaintext, with the encrypted signature appended to it in order to verify the source.)

When secrecy as well as verification is a matter of importance, the message may in effect be sealed by adding a layer of encryption to the signed message, as shown below. After encrypting the message with his private key (signing it), John Smith applies the receiver's—in this instance, Julia Edwards'—public key to the ciphertext, sealing it from any eyes but hers. To render the message intelligible, Julia Edwards

must go through a similar two-step procedure. First she must decrypt the transmission with her private key, to undo the seal; then she has to apply John Smith's public key, revealing the message and, in the process, verifying that the message was indeed transmitted by John Smith.

Despite its strength as a cipher and its antiforgery feature, the public-key system demands a certain amount of vigilance on the part of its users. Although public keys could theoretically be broadcast to all the world, they are normally made available only to the members of the network in which they are used; this prevents an outsider from even attempting forgery. Access to public keys can be restricted by keeping them in a protected directory or in a protected computer file (pages 73-85). Private keys, of course, must be protected with even more stringent precautions, else both secrecy and verification are nullified.

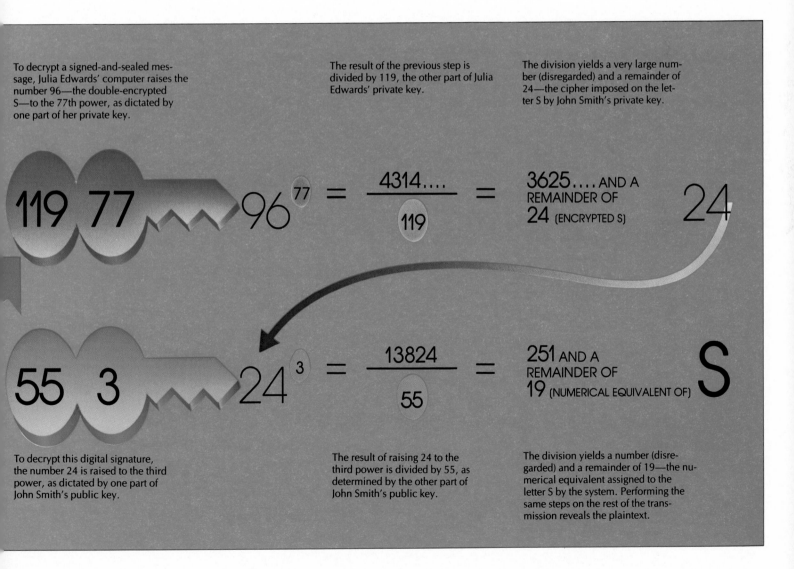

To decrypt a signed-and-sealed message, Julia Edwards' computer raises the number 96—the double-encrypted S—to the 77th power, as dictated by one part of her private key.

The result of the previous step is divided by 119, the other part of Julia Edwards' private key.

The division yields a very large number (disregarded) and a remainder of 24—the cipher imposed on the letter S by John Smith's private key.

$$119 \quad 77 \quad 96^{77} = \frac{4314....}{119} = 3625.... \text{ AND A REMAINDER OF } 24 \text{ (ENCRYPTED S)} \quad 24$$

$$55 \quad 3 \quad 24^{3} = \frac{13824}{55} = 251 \text{ AND A REMAINDER OF } 19 \text{ (NUMERICAL EQUIVALENT OF) } S$$

To decrypt this digital signature, the number 24 is raised to the third power, as dictated by one part of John Smith's public key.

The result of raising 24 to the third power is divided by 55, as determined by the other part of John Smith's public key.

The division yields a number (disregarded) and a remainder of 19—the numerical equivalent assigned to the letter S by the system. Performing the same steps on the rest of the transmission reveals the plaintext.

Glossary

Access control: the use of either physical safeguards such as locks or software safeguards such as passwords to prevent unauthorized access to a computer.

Access-control list: a list of users who are allowed access to a program or data file, including the extent of each user's authorized access; *see* read-access and write-access.

Algorithm: a step-by-step procedure for solving a problem; in encryption, the mathematical procedure used to create a cipher.

Amplifier: an electronic device that increases the voltage or power level of a signal.

Analog: the representation of changes in a continuous physical variable (sound, for example) by continuous changes in another physical variable (such as electrical current).

Analog-to-digital converter: a device that changes an analog signal into digital information.

Analytical attack: an attempt to break a code or cipher key by discovering flaws in its encryption algorithm; *see also* brute-force attack.

Assembly language: a low-level programming language, just above the zeros and ones of machine code, that employs short mnemonic codes to tell the computer to carry out operations.

Audit trail: a chronological record of computer activity automatically maintained to trace all use of the computer; for security purposes, it is preferable that the record be maintained by the operating system.

Authentication: the process of establishing the validity of a message or of verifying a user's authorization for access to data.

Backup facility: a guarded building whose climate-controlled vaults contain copies of data and software.

Bit: the smallest unit of information in a binary computer, represented by a single zero or one. The word "bit" is a contraction of "binary digit."

Black box: a homemade electronic device that stops the signal indicating a completed telephone call so that the call does not trigger billing machinery; *see also* phone phreaking.

Blue box: a homemade electronic device that synthesizes single-frequency telephone-dialing tones to defeat long-distance billing machinery.

Browsing: *see* scavenging.

Brute-force attack: a computerized trial-and-error attempt to decode a cipher by trying every possible key; also called exhaustive attack.

Cable: a group of insulated conductors encased in a protective sheath.

Callback routine: a method of controlling telephone access to a computer with a device that registers an authorized password, then hangs up and calls back to that user's authorized phone number.

Central office: local telephone-switching equipment for a given geographic area.

Channel: an electronic communications path within a computer system or in telecommunications between systems.

Checksum: results of mathematical computations involving the bits in a sector on a floppy disk; used to verify sector accuracy.

Cipher: an encryption system that arbitrarily represents each character by one or more other characters.

Ciphertext: the encrypted, unintelligible text produced by a cipher.

Circuit: a closed network through which current can flow.

Code: an encryption system whose components represent characters, words or sentences.

Cold site: a backup facility that has been equipped with communications gear, computer cables and air conditioning, so that it is possible to install computers quickly in case of disaster at the primary site.

Computer network: a system of two or more computers connected by communications channels.

Cryptography: the enciphering and deciphering of messages using secret ciphers or codes.

Data diddling: unauthorized alteration of data as it is entered or stored in a computer.

Data Encryption Standard (DES): a single-key system selected by the U.S. National Bureau of Standards for encryption of commercial data.

Data leakage: the theft of data or software.

Decryption: using the appropriate key to convert ciphertext to plaintext.

Degausser: a device whose strong magnetic field erases disks and tapes so that they can be reused or discarded.

Demultiplexer: a circuit that separates one input signal from multiple accompanying signals and distributes it to an output line; *see also* multiplexer.

Digital: pertaining to the representation, manipulation or transmission of information by discrete, or on-off, signals.

Digital signature: a verification method in public-key ciphers in which the message is encrypted with the sender's private key and the recipient decrypts the signature with the sender's public key.

Disaster-recovery plan (DRP): a prearranged procedure to quickly transfer backup programs and data to a backup computer in case of catastrophic damage to a primary computer.

Disk: a round magnetic plate—or a stack of such plates—usually made of plastic or metal, used for data storage.

Disk drive: the mechanism that rotates a storage disk and reads or records data.

Eavesdropping: unauthorized interception of data transmissions.

Electromagnetic emanations: data-bearing signals radiated through the air or through conductors.

Electromagnetic pulse (EMP): the surge of electromagnetic energy generated by a nuclear explosion, which can disable or destroy computers and other transistorized devices.

Electronic funds transfer (EFT): a computerized transaction, conducted via long-distance telephone lines, that instantly moves money between computer accounts.

Encryption: scrambling data or messages with a cipher or code so that they are unreadable without a secret key.

Exhaustive attack: *see* brute-force attack.

File: a collection of related information stored in a computer.

Frequency: the rate in cycles per second at which an electronic signal is repeated.

Hacker: a computer enthusiast; also, one who seeks to gain unauthorized access to computer systems.

Head crash: a catastrophic malfunction in a hard-disk drive, during which the electronic read/write head touches the rapidly spinning disk, gouging its magnetic surface and destroying both its data and the head.

Hot site: a backup facility equipped with functioning computers.

Key: a sequence of symbols used to encrypt and decrypt data.

Key-distribution center: a communications facility in a single-key encryption network that translates a session key encrypted by a message sender into one encrypted with the recipient's key, allowing secure electronic transmission of keys.

Logic bomb: malicious action, initiated by software, that inhibits normal system functions; a logic bomb takes effect only when specified conditions occur.

Magnetic tape: plastic tape coated with a magnetic material that stores information in the form of magnetized particles.

Mantrap: a booth between an unsecure area and a secure area such as a computer facility, which consists of a pair of electronically controlled doors; the door to the secure area opens only when the user has passed an identity test and the other door has locked.

Message Authentication Code (MAC): a component of the Data Encryption Standard (DES) used to ensure that a message has not been altered.

Modem: a modulator/demodulator device that enables data to be transmitted between computers, generally over telephone lines but sometimes on fiber-optic cable or radio frequencies.

Motor-generator set: an electric motor that drives an electrical generator, which in turn supplies stable power to a mainframe computer, guarding against voltage transients.

Multiplexer: a circuit that transmits several signals simultaneously on a single output channel or wire; *see also* demultiplexer.

One-time pad: a cipher system that uses a notepad of separate ciphers that represent each character of a message as a long series of randomly selected digits. Sender and receiver possess identical pads; each cipher is used only once, then destroyed.

Operating system: a complex set of programs that controls, assists and supervises all other programs run on a computer.

Parity: a bit that indicates whether the number of ones in a bit string is odd or even.

Password: a user's secret sequence of keyboard characters, which must be entered at the beginning of each computer session to verify the user's identity.

Permutation: encrypting data or messages by rearranging the order of their characters; also known as transposition.

Phone phreaking: electronically manipulating telephone signals to deceive billing computers and thus avoid paying for long-distance calls.

Piggybacking: gaining illicit access to a computer facility by following an authorized employee through a controlled door; also known as tailgating.

Plaintext: intelligible text or signals that do not require decryption.

Port: the connection between a computer and another device through which data enters and leaves.

Port protection device (PPD): a microprocessor-driven box that answers a telephone and requires a valid password before connecting a caller to the computer.

Public-key system: a cipher that usually employs a pair of mathematically related keys, one that is public knowledge within the computer network, the other known only to its owner. The sender uses the receiver's public key to encrypt data, which may be decrypted only with the related private key.

Read-access: a user's authorization to read information stored in a computer file.

Reference monitor: a tamperproof operating-system program that classifies users and files, checks each access attempt for proper authorization and denies access to unauthorized users.

Risk analysis: a mathematical method that is used to rank physical and human threats to computers and to their programs and data.

RSA system: a public-key cipher for commercial data that is based on the products of prime numbers; the initials stand for Rivest, Shamir and Adleman, the system's designers.

Scavenging: randomly searching for valuable data in a computer's memory or in discarded or incompletely erased magnetic disks and tapes.

Secret key: a recipient's private key in a public-key system.

Sector: a defined portion of a concentric track on a magnetic disk.

Security filter: a set of software programs that prevents data from being transmitted to unauthorized users or over unprotected communications links.

Session key: the key used to encrypt a single message; *see* key-distribution center.

Single-key system: a cipher that encrypts and decrypts data with the same key.

Software: instructions, or programs, designed to be carried out by a computer.

Substitution: a method for encrypting text or data by substituting different characters for the original ones.

Surge suppressor: a protective electronic circuit for desktop computers that damps voltage transients.

Terminal: a device composed of a keyboard for putting data into a computer and a video screen or printer for receiving data from the computer.

Time bomb: an unauthorized program that takes effect on a specified future date.

Time sharing: the simultaneous use of a computer by more than one person in a multi-user network.

Track: a concentric band on a magnetic disk that contains a specified amount of data.

Transducer: a device that converts one type of energy to another.

Transients: momentary, destructive fluctuations in the voltage supplied to a computer.

Transmitter: a device that sends data over a communications link; also, a device that translates electronic signals into electromagnetic waves.

Transposition: *see* permutation.

Trap door: a set of special instructions, originally created for testing and troubleshooting, that bypasses security procedures and allows direct access to a computer's operating system or to other software.

Trojan horse: a program, purporting to accomplish useful work, that conceals instructions to breach security whenever the software is invoked.

Uninterruptible power supply (UPS): a complex network of electronic circuitry and storage batteries that filters out transients and provides virtually instantaneous backup power in case of blackout.

Virus: a program that copies itself into new data bases and computers whenever its parent program is invoked.

Voltage: a measure of the force that causes electrical current to flow through a circuit.

Wiretapping: monitoring or recording data as it moves across a communications link.

Work factor: an estimate of the time or effort needed to break a code, cipher or other security measure.

Worm: a program that deletes data from a computer's memory.

Write-access: authorization to record or alter data stored in a computer.

The Language of Bits

When confidential data is encrypted for transmission or storage (pages 103-117), both the data and the key used to encode it are converted to strings of bits, the binary digits one and zero, which represent the on-off electronic pulses that are a computer's real language. Depending on what the machine has been programmed to expect, the same sequence of zeros and ones—1000001, say—may represent the decimal value 65 or the roman letter A. (A similar string may represent neither a number nor a letter but instead be an instruction to the computer to add or subtract; a series of such strings could tell the computer to color the screen red.)

At far left is a table listing the binary number system's seven-bit equivalents for the decimal values 0 through 127. As illustrated in the small tables at near left, the value of a binary digit is determined by where it stands in relation to other digits in the string, just as in the decimal system.

Although the binary equivalents of decimal numbers are mathematically based, the binary codes for the characters on a keyboard are arbitrary. In theory, any string of ones and zeros could represent a character; in practice, standard representations have been devised to enable computers to perform useful operations such as alphabetizing. The convention also allows computers to communicate electronically with one another and with a variety of peripheral devices, such as keyboards and printers. At near left is a partial list of the binary code for alphabetic and numeric characters as established by the American Standard Code for Information Interchange (ASCII). ASCII assigns a string of seven bits—plus another bit for checking purposes (below)—to each upper- and lower-case letter of the alphabet, to the 10 decimal symbols, and to punctuation marks and control characters (for keyboard or printer functions, such as carriage return or backspace). ASCII is the most widely used convention in the United States; other countries employ modified international versions.

In a decimal number, each column to the left increases in value by the power of 10: 1, 10, 100, 1,000 and so on. An individual number is the sum of the values of its place columns. Here, one 100, no 10s and nine 1s equals 109.

PLACE 100	PLACE 10	PLACE 1
1	0	9

$$100 + 0 + 9 = 109$$

In binary, the value of each column to the left increases by the power of two: 1, 2, 4 and so on. Only two symbols, 1 and 0, mark place values. Here, one 64, one 32, no 16s, one 8, one 4, no 2s and one 1 combine to equal 109.

PLACE 64	PLACE 32	PLACE 16	PLACE 8	PLACE 4	PLACE 2	PLACE 1
1	1	0	1	1	0	1

$$64 + 32 + 0 + 8 + 4 + 0 + 1 = 109$$

DECIMAL NUMBER / BINARY EQUIVALENT

DECIMAL NUMBER (100 10 1)	64	32	16	8	4	2	1
0	0	0	0	0	0	0	0
1	0	0	0	0	0	0	1
2	0	0	0	0	0	1	0
3	0	0	0	0	0	1	1
4	0	0	0	0	1	0	0
5	0	0	0	0	1	0	1
6	0	0	0	0	1	1	0
7	0	0	0	0	1	1	1
8	0	0	0	1	0	0	0
9	0	0	0	1	0	0	1
10	0	0	0	1	0	1	0
11	0	0	0	1	0	1	1
12	0	0	0	1	1	0	0
13	0	0	0	1	1	0	1
14	0	0	0	1	1	1	0
15	0	0	0	1	1	1	1
16	0	0	1	0	0	0	0
17	0	0	1	0	0	0	1
18	0	0	1	0	0	1	0
19	0	0	1	0	0	1	1
20	0	0	1	0	1	0	0
21	0	0	1	0	1	0	1
22	0	0	1	0	1	1	0
23	0	0	1	0	1	1	1
24	0	0	1	1	0	0	0
25	0	0	1	1	0	0	1
26	0	0	1	1	0	1	0
27	0	0	1	1	0	1	1
28	0	0	1	1	1	0	0
29	0	0	1	1	1	0	1
30	0	0	1	1	1	1	0
31	0	0	1	1	1	1	1
32	0	1	0	0	0	0	0
33	0	1	0	0	0	0	1
34	0	1	0	0	0	1	0
35	0	1	0	0	0	1	1
36	0	1	0	0	1	0	0
37	0	1	0	0	1	0	1
38	0	1	0	0	1	1	0
39	0	1	0	0	1	1	1
40	0	1	0	1	0	0	0
41	0	1	0	1	0	0	1
42	0	1	0	1	0	1	0
43	0	1	0	1	0	1	1
44	0	1	0	1	1	0	0
45	0	1	0	1	1	0	1
46	0	1	0	1	1	1	0
47	0	1	0	1	1	1	1
48	0	1	1	0	0	0	0
49	0	1	1	0	0	0	1
50	0	1	1	0	0	1	0
51	0	1	1	0	0	1	1
52	0	1	1	0	1	0	0
53	0	1	1	0	1	0	1
54	0	1	1	0	1	1	0
55	0	1	1	0	1	1	1
56	0	1	1	1	0	0	0
57	0	1	1	1	0	0	1
58	0	1	1	1	0	1	0
59	0	1	1	1	0	1	1

ASCII CODE

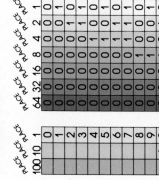

(space)	0	1	0	0	0	0	0	0
!	0	1	0	0	0	0	0	1
"	0	1	0	0	0	0	1	0
#	0	1	0	0	0	0	1	1
$	0	1	0	0	0	1	0	0
%	0	1	0	0	0	1	0	1
&	0	1	0	0	0	1	1	0
'	0	1	0	0	0	1	1	1
(	0	1	0	0	1	0	0	0
)	0	1	0	0	1	0	0	1
*	0	1	0	0	1	0	1	0
+	0	1	0	0	1	0	1	1
,	0	1	0	0	1	1	0	0
-	0	1	0	0	1	1	0	1
.	0	1	0	0	1	1	1	0
/	0	1	0	0	1	1	1	1
0	0	1	0	1	0	0	0	0
1	0	1	0	1	0	0	0	1
2	0	1	0	1	0	0	1	0
3	0	1	0	1	0	0	1	1
4	0	1	0	1	0	1	0	0
5	0	1	0	1	0	1	0	1
6	0	1	0	1	0	1	1	0
7	0	1	0	1	0	1	1	1
8	0	1	0	1	1	0	0	1
9	0	1	0	1	1	0	0	1
:	0	1	0	1	1	0	1	0
;	0	1	0	1	1	0	1	1

Dec		Binary (7 bits)							ASCII	Binary (7 bits)						
6	4	1	0	0	0	0	0	0	@	1	0	0	0	0	0	0
6	5	1	0	0	0	0	0	1	A	1	0	0	0	0	0	1
6	6	1	0	0	0	0	1	0	B	1	0	0	0	0	1	0
6	7	1	0	0	0	0	1	1	C	1	0	0	0	0	1	1
6	8	1	0	0	0	1	0	0	D	1	0	0	0	1	0	0
6	9	1	0	0	0	1	0	1	E	1	0	0	0	1	0	1
7	0	1	0	0	0	1	1	0	F	1	0	0	0	1	1	0
7	1	1	0	0	0	1	1	1	G	1	0	0	0	1	1	1
7	2	1	0	0	1	0	0	0	H	1	0	0	1	0	0	0
7	3	1	0	0	1	0	0	1	I	1	0	0	1	0	0	1
7	4	1	0	0	1	0	1	0	J	1	0	0	1	0	1	0
7	5	1	0	0	1	0	1	1	K	1	0	0	1	0	1	1
7	6	1	0	0	1	1	0	0	L	1	0	0	1	1	0	0
7	7	1	0	0	1	1	0	1	M	1	0	0	1	1	0	1
7	8	1	0	0	1	1	1	0	N	1	0	0	1	1	1	0
7	9	1	0	0	1	1	1	1	O	1	0	0	1	1	1	1
8	0	1	0	1	0	0	0	0	P	1	0	1	0	0	0	0
8	1	1	0	1	0	0	0	1	Q	1	0	1	0	0	0	1
8	2	1	0	1	0	0	1	0	R	1	0	1	0	0	1	0
8	3	1	0	1	0	0	1	1	S	1	0	1	0	0	1	1
8	4	1	0	1	0	1	0	0	T	1	0	1	0	1	0	0
8	5	1	0	1	0	1	0	1	U	1	0	1	0	1	0	1
8	6	1	0	1	0	1	1	0	V	1	0	1	0	1	1	0
8	7	1	0	1	0	1	1	1	W	1	0	1	0	1	1	1
8	8	1	0	1	1	0	0	0	X	1	0	1	1	0	0	0
8	9	1	0	1	1	0	0	1	Y	1	0	1	1	0	0	1
9	0	1	0	1	1	0	1	0	Z	1	0	1	1	0	1	0
9	1	1	0	1	1	0	1	1	[	1	0	1	1	0	1	1
9	2	1	0	1	1	1	0	0	\	1	0	1	1	1	0	0
9	3	1	0	1	1	1	0	1	]	1	0	1	1	1	0	1
9	4	1	0	1	1	1	1	0	^	1	0	1	1	1	1	0
9	5	1	0	1	1	1	1	1	_	1	0	1	1	1	1	1
9	6	1	1	0	0	0	0	0	'	1	1	0	0	0	0	0
9	7	1	1	0	0	0	0	1	a	1	1	0	0	0	0	1
9	8	1	1	0	0	0	1	0	b	1	1	0	0	0	1	0
9	9	1	1	0	0	0	1	1	c	1	1	0	0	0	1	1
1	0 0	1	1	0	0	1	0	0	d	1	1	0	0	1	0	0
1	0 1	1	1	0	0	1	0	1	e	1	1	0	0	1	0	1
1	0 2	1	1	0	0	1	1	0	f	1	1	0	0	1	1	0
1	0 3	1	1	0	0	1	1	1	g	1	1	0	0	1	1	1
1	0 4	1	1	0	1	0	0	0	h	1	1	0	1	0	0	0
1	0 5	1	1	0	1	0	0	1	i	1	1	0	1	0	0	1
1	0 6	1	1	0	1	0	1	0	j	1	1	0	1	0	1	0
1	0 7	1	1	0	1	0	1	1	k	1	1	0	1	0	1	1
1	0 8	1	1	0	1	1	0	0	l	1	1	0	1	1	0	0
1	0 9	1	1	0	1	1	0	1	m	1	1	0	1	1	0	1
1	1 0	1	1	0	1	1	1	0	n	1	1	0	1	1	1	0
1	1 1	1	1	0	1	1	1	1	o	1	1	0	1	1	1	1
1	1 2	1	1	1	0	0	0	0	p	1	1	1	0	0	0	0
1	1 3	1	1	1	0	0	0	1	q	1	1	1	0	0	0	1
1	1 4	1	1	1	0	0	1	0	r	1	1	1	0	0	1	0
1	1 5	1	1	1	0	0	1	1	s	1	1	1	0	0	1	1
1	1 6	1	1	1	0	1	0	0	t	1	1	1	0	1	0	0
1	1 7	1	1	1	0	1	0	1	u	1	1	1	0	1	0	1
1	1 8	1	1	1	0	1	1	0	v	1	1	1	0	1	1	0
1	1 9	1	1	1	0	1	1	1	w	1	1	1	0	1	1	1
1	2 0	1	1	1	1	0	0	0	x	1	1	1	1	0	0	0
1	2 1	1	1	1	1	0	0	1	y	1	1	1	1	0	0	1
1	2 2	1	1	1	1	0	1	0	z	1	1	1	1	0	1	0
1	2 3	1	1	1	1	0	1	1	{	1	1	1	1	0	1	1
1	2 4	1	1	1	1	1	0	0	|	1	1	1	1	1	0	0
1	2 5	1	1	1	1	1	0	1	}	1	1	1	1	1	0	1
1	2 6	1	1	1	1	1	1	0	~	1	1	1	1	1	1	0
1	2 7	1	1	1	1	1	1	1	DEL	1	1	1	1	1	1	1

At far left are the 128 possible combinations of one and zero in a seven-bit string—the equivalents of the decimal numbers 0 through 127. At near left, starting with the binary equivalent of 32, are 96 of the same strings as they are used in ASCII to designate keyboard characters. The ASCII list actually begins with 32 codes for control functions, such as carriage return and backspace; it ends with a code for the delete function.

An Extra Bit for Parity

In addition to the seven bits used to encode binary numbers and ASCII characters, each string may have an extra bit space, normally reserved for a checking mechanism known as a parity bit. A parity bit is like a flag that signals whether errors have occurred during the transmission of data from one computer to another. A computer transmits data in either odd or even parity. Odd parity means that each bit string must have an odd number of ones; during transmission, the computer places either a one or a zero in the string's unused bit space to make the total number of ones odd. The receiving computer then checks to see if the number of ones it receives matches the message's parity designation. Usually the leftmost bit space is reserved for a parity bit, as with the ASCII code for *B*, below. In rare cases, as with the Data Encryption Standard key on page 108, the rightmost space is used; in the example at bottom, the binary equivalent of the decimal number one is followed by an extra zero for odd parity.

PLACE	PLACE	PLACE	PLACE	PLACE	PLACE	PLACE
	64	32	16	8	4	2	1

1	1	0	0	0	0	1	0

0	0	0	0	0	0	1	0

Bibliography

Books

Beker, Henry, and Fred Piper, *Cipher Systems*. New York: John Wiley and Sons, 1982.

Bosworth, Bruce, *Codes, Ciphers, and Computers*. New York: Hayden Book Company, Inc., 1982.

Burnham, David, *The Rise of the Computer State*. New York: Random House, 1983.

Castleman, Kenneth R., *Digital Image Processing*. Englewood Cliffs, N.J.: Prentice-Hall, 1979.

Computer Piracy and Privacy (Home of the Future: Industry Research Report series). Boston: The Yankee Group, 1984.

Cooper, James Arlin, *Computer-Security Technology*. Lexington, Mass.: Lexington Books, 1984.

Davies, D. W., and W. L. Price, *Security for Computer Networks*. New York: John Wiley & Sons, 1984.

Deavours, Cipher A., and Louis Kruh, *Machine Cryptography and Modern Cryptanalysis*. Dedham, Mass.: Artech House, 1985.

The Electronic Vault: Computer Piracy and Privacy. (Home of the Future: Industry Research Report series). Boston: The Yankee Group, 1984.

Fike, John L., and George E. Friend, *Understanding Telephone Electronics*. Dallas, Tex.: Texas Instruments Incorporated, 1983.

Hemphill, Charles F., Jr., and Robert D. Hemphill, *Security Safeguards for the Computer*. New York: AMACOM, 1979.

Hsiao, David K., Douglas S. Kerr and Stuart E. Madnick, *Computer Security*. New York: Academic Press, 1979.

Kahn, David:
  The Codebreakers. New York: Macmillan Company, 1967.
  Kahn on Codes. New York: Macmillan Company, 1983.

Katzen, Harry, Jr., *The Standard Data Encryption Algorithm*. New York: Petrocelli Books, 1977.

Lavington, Simon, *Early British Computers*. Manchester, England: Manchester University Press, 1980.

Lewin, Ronald, *Ultra Goes to War*. New York: McGraw-Hill, 1978.

Metropolis, N., J. Howlett and Gian-Carlo Rota, eds., *A History of Computing in the Twentieth Century: A Collection of Essays*. New York: Academic Press, 1980.

Meyer, Carl H., and Stephen M. Matyas, *Cryptography: A New Dimension in Computer Data Security*. New York: John Wiley & Sons, 1982.

Norman, Adrian R. D., *Computer Insecurity*. London: Chapman and Hall, 1983.

Parker, Donn B.:
  Crime by Computer. New York: Charles Scribner's Sons, 1976.
  Fighting Computer Crime. New York: Charles Scribner's Sons, 1983.

Pierce, John R., and Edward E. David Jr., *Man's World of Sound*. Garden City, N.Y.: Doubleday, 1958.

Shurkin, Joel, *Engines of the Mind*. New York: W. W. Norton & Company, 1984.

Troy, Eugene F., Stuart W. Katzke and Dennis D. Steinauer, *Technical Solutions to the Computer Security Intrusion Problem*. Washington, D.C.: National Science Foundation, 1984.

Turn, Rein, ed., *Advances in Computer System Security*. Vol. 2. Dedham, Mass.: Artech House, 1984.

Walker, Roger S., *Understanding Computer Science*. Dallas, Tex.: Texas Instruments Learning Center, 1981.

Welchman, Gordon, *Breaking the Enigma Codes*. New York: McGraw-Hill, 1982.

Whiteside, Thomas, *Computer Capers*. New York: Thomas Y. Crowell Company, 1978.

Zaks, Rodnay, and Austin Lesea, *Microprocessor Interfacing Techniques*. Berkeley, Calif.: Sybex, 1979.

Periodicals

Armor, John C., "Computer Bandits Should Be Outlawed." *Newsday*, August 30, 1983.

Baird, Lindsay L., "Sensible Network Security." *Datamation*, February 1, 1985.

Beker, Henry, and Fred Piper, "Cryptography for Beginners." *New Scientist*, July 1983.

Bernhard, Robert, "Breaching System Security." *IEEE Spectrum*, June 1982.

"Biometric Security Systems." *Data Processing & Communications Security*, Vol. 8, No. 6, no date.

Block, David, "The Trapdoor Algorithm." *Creative Computing*, May 1983.

Boebert, W. E., R. Y. Kain and W. D. Young, "Secure Computing: The Secure Ada Target Approach." *Scientific Honeyweller*, July 1985.

Browne, Malcolm W., "Locking Out the Hackers." *Discover*, November 1983.

Cannon, T. M., and B. R. Hunt, "Image Processing by Computer." *Scientific American*, October 1981.

Chenoweth, Karin, "Libraries Survive the Ides of March." *The Montgomery Journal* (Montgomery County, Md.), March 18, 1982.

Cohen, Laurie P., "Internal Security." *The Wall Street Journal*, September 16, 1985.

Colby, Wendelin, "Burnt or Burned." *Infosystems*, February 1985.

Cook, Rick, "Power Line Protection." *Popular Computing*, November 1984.

"Cracking Down on Crime." *Datamation*, May 1, 1985.

Dembart, Lee, "Attack of the Computer Virus." *Discover*, November 1984.

Dewdney, A. K., "Computer Recreations." *Scientific American*, September 1985.

DiNucci, Darcy, "Copying Software: Who's Right?" *PC World*, Vol. 3, Issue 9, no date.

Downs, Deborah D., "Operating Systems Key Security with Basic Software Mechanisms." *Electronics*, March 8, 1984.

Edersheim, Peggy, "Computer Crime." *The Wall Street Journal*, August 15, 1985.

Flowers, Thomas H., "The Design of Colossus." *Annals of the History of Computing*, July 1983.

Gillard, Collen, and Jim Smith, "Computer Crime: A Growing Threat." *BYTE*, October 1983.

Gorney, Cynthia, "Hack Attack." *The Washington Post*, December 6, 1984.

Hellman, Martin E., "The Mathematics of Public-Key Cryptography." *Scientific American*, August 1979.

"His Master's (Digital) Voice." *Time*, April 1, 1985.

Horgan, John, "Thwarting the Information Thieves." *IEEE Spectrum*, July 1985.

Howitt, Doran, "Of Worms and Booby Traps." *InfoWorld*, November 19, 1984.

Immel, A. Richard, "Data Security." *Popular Computing*, May 1984.

"Innovations: Patents, Processes, and Products." *IEEE Spectrum,* October 1985.

Janulartis, Victor:
"Creating a Disaster Recovery Plan." *Infosystems,* February 1985.
"Getting a Grip on Disaster Planning Needs." *Infosystems,* February 1985.

"Key Proposal: ADAPSO Seeks a Hardware Solution to Piracy." *Business Computer Systems,* February 1985.

Kolata, Gina:
"Computer Break-Ins Fan Security Fears." *Science,* September 2, 1983.
"Scheme to Foil Software Pirates." *Science,* September 23, 1983.
"When Criminals Turn to Computers, Is Anything Safe?" *Smithsonian,* August 1982.

Larson, Harry T., "Who Goes There?" *Hardcopy,* March 1985.

Leadabrand, Russ, "Thwarting Computer Thieves." *Computer Merchandising,* November 1983.

McLellen, Vin, "Phone Phink: A Super-Hacker Turns State's Evidence." *Digital Review,* January 1985.

Mager, Gary, "Saving Your Computer from Surges, Sags or Noise." *The DEC Professional,* December 1984.

Marbach, William D., et al., "Beware: Hackers at Play." *Newsweek,* September 5, 1983.

Markoff, John, Phillip Robinson and Ezra Shapiro, "Up to Date." *BYTE,* March 1985.

Maude, Tim, and Derwent Maude, "Hardware Protection against Software Piracy." *Communications of the ACM,* September 1984.

Murphy, Jamie, "A Threat from Malicious Software." *Time,* November 4, 1985.

Myers, Edith, "Speaking in Codes." *Datamation,* December 1, 1984.

"New Code Is Broken." *Science,* May 1982.

Ognibene, Peter J.:
"Computer Saboteurs." *Science Digest,* July 1984.
"Secret Ciphers Solved: Artificial Intelligence." *OMNI,* November 1984.

Rapoport, Roger, "Unbreakable Code." *OMNI,* September 1980.

Rosch, Winn L., "PC Data Is Vulnerable to Attack." *PC Magazine,* July 23, 1985.

Sandza, Richard, "The Night of the Hackers." *Newsweek,* November 12, 1984.

Schlosberg, Jeremy, "Out of Site." *Digital Review,* March 1985.

Schrager, Barry, "Outwitting 2-Bit Thieves and Arresting Computer Crime." *Data Communications,* November 1982.

"Security and Vax/VMS." *The DEC Professional,* December 1984.

Shannon, Terry C., "Computer Security—a Checklist." *The DEC Professional,* December 1984.

Small, David, "The Futility of Copy Protection." *Tech Journal,* December 1985.

Smiddy, James D., and Linda O. Smiddy, "Caught in the Act." *Datamation,* June 15, 1985.

Smith, Jim:
"Call-Back Schemes Ward Off Unwanted Access by Telephone." *Electronics,* March 8, 1984.
"Callback Security System Prevents Unauthorized Computer Access." *Mini-Micro Systems,* July 1984.

Solomon, Les, and Stan Veit, "Data Storage in a Nutshell."

Computers & Electronics, July 1983.

"The Spreading Danger of Computer Crime." *Business Week,* April 20, 1981.

Sullivan, Joseph, "Cryptography: Securing Computer Transmissions." *High Technology,* November 1983.

"Taking a Byte out of Crime." *Time,* October 14, 1985.

Thé, Lee, "Controlling Access to Your Data." *Personal Computing,* September 1985.

Thornton, Mary, " 'Hackers' Ignore Consequences of Their High-Tech Joy Rides." *The Washington Post,* May 2, 1984.

"A Threat from Malicious Software." *Time,* November 4, 1985.

Troy, Gene, "Thwarting the Hackers: New Security Protection Devices." *Datamation,* July 1, 1984.

Tubb, Phillip, "A Layman's Guide to Disk Protection." *Creative Computing,* July 1983.

"Vault Delays 'Worm' Plan." *InfoWorld,* January 21, 1985.

Wellborn, Stanley N., "Foolproof ID: Opening Locks with Your Body." *U.S. News & World Report,* December 17, 1984.

Wong, Kenneth, "Computer Disaster in the United Kingdom." *Edpacs,* January 1985.

Zimmerman, Joel, "Is Your Computer Insecure?" *Datamation,* May 15, 1985.

Other Publications

Association of Data Processing Service Organizations (ADAPSO), *Proposal for Software Authorization System Standards,* August 16, 1985.

"Background Press Information." Beaverton, Ore.: EyeDentify, Inc., no date.

Barton, Ben F., and Marthalee S. Barton, "User-Friendly Password Methods for Computer-Mediated Information Systems." *Computers & Security 3,* Amsterdam, the Netherlands: Elsevier Science Publishers B. V., 1984.

Branstad, Dennis K., and Miles E. Smid, "Integrity and Security Standards Based on Cryptography." *Computers & Security 1,* Amsterdam, the Netherlands: Elsevier Science Publishers, B. V., 1982.

Cohen, Fred, "Computer Viruses: Theory and Experiments." 7th DOD/NBS Computer Security Conference, September 1984.

Colvin, Bill D., "Computer Crime Investigators: A New Training Field." *FBI Law Enforcement Bulletin,* July 1979.

"Computer Crime." *Criminal Justice Resource Manual.* Washington, D.C.: Bureau of Justice Statistics/U.S. Department of Justice, 1979.

"Data Encryption Standard." *Federal Information Processing Standards Publication 46.* Washington, D.C.: U.S. Department of Commerce/National Bureau of Standards, January 15, 1977.

"The EyeDentification System 7.5: Health, Safety and Statistical Performance Review." Beaverton, Ore.: EyeDentify, Inc., December 1984.

Government Computer News, September 27, 1985.

"Guidelines for Automatic Data Processing Physical Security and Risk Management." *Federal Information Processing Standards Publication 31.* Washington, D.C.: U.S. Department of Commerce/National Bureau of Standards, June 1974.

"Guidelines for Implementing and Using the NBS Data Encryption Standard." *Federal Information Processing Standards Publication 74.* Washington, D.C.: U.S. Department of Commerce/National Bureau of Standards, April 1, 1981.

"Guidelines on Evaluation of Techniques for Automated Personal Identification." *Federal Information Processing Standards Publication 48*. Washington, D.C.: U.S. Department of Commerce/ National Bureau of Standards, April 1, 1977.

"Guidelines on User Authentication Techniques for Computer Network Access Control." *Federal Information Processing Standards Publication 83*. Washington, D.C.: U.S. Department of Commerce/National Bureau of Standards, September 1980.

Henkel, Tom, and Peter Bartolik, eds., "Protecting the Corporate Data Resource." Special Report, *Computerworld*, November 28, 1983.

Herschberg, I. S., and R. Paans, "The Programmer's Threat: Cases and Causes." *Computers & Security 3*. Amsterdam, the Netherlands: Elsevier Science Publishers B. V., 1984.

Murray, William H., "Computer Security: Observations on the State of the Technology." *Computers & Security 2*, Amsterdam, the Netherlands: Elsevier Science Publishers B. V., 1983.

Sanders, C. W., et al., *Study of Vulnerability of Electronic Communication Systems to Electronic Interception*. McLean, Va.: The Mitre Corporation, January 1977.

Schell, Roger R., "Computer Security: The Achilles' Heel of the Electronic Air Force?" *Air University Review*, January-February 1979.

"Security of Personal Computer Systems: A Management Guide." *NBS Special Publication 500-120*, Institute for Computer Sciences and Technology, National Bureau of Standards, no date.

Smid, Miles E., "Integrating the Data Encryption Standard into Computer Networks." *IEEE Transactions on Communications*, June 1981.

Steinauer, Dennis D., *Security of Personal Computers: A Growing Concern*. Washington, D.C.: National Bureau of Standards, no date.

Stokes, Robert S., "Scam-Free S.W.I.F.T. Net May Not Be 'Sting'-Proof." *Management Information Systems Week*, Vol. 3, No. 28, no date.

Tangney, John D., "History of Protection in Computer Systems." *MITRE Technical Report*. The Mitre Corporation, 1981.

Thompson, Phil, Alan Silver and Michael Brown, *Copy II Plus*. Portland, Ore.: Central Point Software, Inc., no date.

Troy, Eugene F., "Dial-Up Security Update." *Proceedings of the 8th National Computer Security Conference*. Gaithersburg, Md. September-October 1985.

Troy, Eugene F., Stuart W. Katzke and Dennis D. Steinauer, *Technical Solutions to the Computer Security Intrusion Problem*. Washington, D.C.: National Bureau of Standards, November 2, 1984.

Turn, Rein, "Private Sector Needs for Trusted/Secure Computer Systems." *Report R-2811-DR&E Trusted Computer Systems: Needs and Incentives for Use in Government and the Private Sector*. The Rand Corporation, June 1981.

Wood, Helen M., *Computer Science & Technology: The Use of Passwords for Controlled Access to Computer Resources*. Washington, D.C.: Institute for Computer Sciences and Technology, National Bureau of Standards, May 1977.

Worthington, T. K., et al., "IBM Dynamic Signature Verification." *Computer Security*. Amsterdam, the Netherlands: Elsevier Science Publishers B. V., 1985.

Acknowledgments

The index for this book was prepared by Mel Ingber. The editors also wish to thank: California—Carlsbad: Helen C. Remington, Allenbach Industries; Mountainview: Robert B. Barnes, Drexler Technology Corporation; Whitfield Diffie, Bell Northern Research Incorporated; Palo Alto: Randall Hawks, Identix Incorporated; San Jose: Alan H. Keating, Stellar Systems; Colorado—Colorado Springs: Virginia Sullivan, North American Aerospace Defense Command; Maryland—Fort Meade: Marvin Schaefer, National Computer Security Center; Gaithersburg: David Balenson, National Bureau of Standards; Owings Mills: John Hynes, Malco Security Magnetics; Massachusetts—Arlington: Ronald Rivest; Cambridge: Daniel Sevush, Lotus Development Corporation; New Mexico—Albuquerque: Russell Maxwell; New York—Yorktown Heights: Thomas Worthington, IBM Corporation; Ohio—Columbus: David Schinke, AT&T Bell Laboratories; Oregon—Portland: Michael Brown, Central Point Software; Steven Flego, Eyedentify Inc.; Pennsylvania—Philadelphia: Ian Murphy, Secure Data Systems; Texas—Dallas: George Doddington, Texas Instruments.

Picture Credits

The sources for the illustrations that appear in this book are listed below. Credits from left to right are separated by semicolons, from top to bottom by dashes.
Cover, 6: Art by Andrea Baruffi. 12-15: Art by Aaron Bowles. 21-25: Art by Steve Wagner. 26: Art by Andrea Baruffi. 31: Art by William J. Hennessy Jr. 36-39: Art by Peter Sawyer. 43: Art by William J. Hennessy Jr. 45-49: Art by Matt McMullen. 50, 51: Art by Matt McMullen—courtesy AT&T Bell Laboratories. 52-57: Art by Matt McMullen. 58-62: Art by Andrea Baruffi. 65-67: Art by Frederic F. Bigio from B-C Graphics. 70-85: Art by William J. Hennessy Jr. 86-91: Art by Andrea Baruffi. 94-97: Art by Wayne Vincent. 103-117: Art by Sam Haltom.

Index

Time-Life Books Inc.
is a wholly owned subsidiary of
TIME INCORPORATED

FOUNDER: Henry R. Luce 1898-1967

Editor-in-Chief: Henry Anatole Grunwald
President: J. Richard Munro
Chairman of the Board: Ralph P. Davidson
Corporate Editor: Ray Cave
Group Vice President, Books: Reginald K. Brack Jr.
Vice President, Books: George Artandi

TIME-LIFE BOOKS INC.

EDITOR: George Constable
Executive Editor: George Daniels
Editorial General Manager: Neal Goff
Director of Design: Louis Klein
Director of Editorial Resources: Phyllis K. Wise
Editorial Board: Dale M. Brown, Roberta Conlan,
Ellen Phillips, Donia Ann Steele, Rosalind Stubenberg,
Kit van Tulleken, Henry Woodhead
Director of Research and Photography:
John Conrad Weiser

PRESIDENT: Reginald K. Brack Jr.
Executive Vice Presidents: John M. Fahey Jr.,
Christopher T. Linen
Senior Vice President: James L. Mercer
Vice Presidents: Stephen L. Bair, Edward Brash,
Ralph J. Cuomo, Juanita T. James, Wilhelm R. Saake,
Robert H. Smith, Paul R. Stewart, Leopoldo Toralballa

Editorial Operations
Copy Chief: Diane Ullius
Editorial Operations: Caroline A. Boubin (manager)
Production: Celia Beattie
Quality Control: James J. Cox (director)
Library: Louise D. Forstall

Correspondents: Elisabeth Kraemer-Singh (Bonn);
Dorothy Bacon (London); Maria Vincenza Aloisi,
Josephine du Brusle (Paris); Ann Natanson (Rome).

UNDERSTANDING COMPUTERS

SERIES DIRECTOR: Roberta Conlan
Series Administrator: Rita Thievon Mullin

Editorial Staff for *Computer Security*
Designer: Ellen Robling
Associate Editors: Lee Hassig (text),
Judith W. Shanks (pictures)
Researchers: Roxie France-Nuriddin, Tina S. McDowell
Writer: Lydia Preston
Assistant Designer: Antonio Alcalá
Copy Coordinators: Anthony K. Pordes,
Jayne E. Rohrich, Robert M. S. Somerville
Picture Coordinator: Renée DeSandies
Editorial Assistant: Miriam Newton Morrison

Special Contributors: (text) Ronald H. Bailey, Sarah
Brash, Richard D. James, John I. Merritt, Charles C.
Smith, David Thiemann; (research) Isabel Fucigna,
Sara Mark

GENERAL CONSULTANT

ISABEL LIDA NIRENBERG has dealt with a wide range of
computer applications, from the analysis of data collected by the Pioneer space probes to the matching of children and families for adoption agencies. She works at the
Computer Center at the State University of New York at
Albany, and assists faculty and students there with micro-
computer applications.

OTHER CONSULTANTS

DR. DENNIS BRANSTAD is a National Bureau of Standards Computer Science Fellow in computer security in
the Institute for Computer Sciences and Technology. He
has been responsible for the development of computer-
security standards for the government and private industry since 1973.

JAMES ARLIN COOPER works at the Sandia National
Laboratories in Albuquerque, New Mexico, and is also an
Adjunct Professor of Electrical Engineering at the Univer-
sity of New Mexico.

DR. STUART KATZKE heads the Computer Security Management and Evaluation Group in the Institute for Computer Sciences and Technology at the National Bureau of
Standards. He is responsible for the development of federal information-processing standards and computer-
security guidelines.

CARL E. LANDWEHR is a computer scientist at the Naval
Research Laboratory. The author of several articles on
computer security, he has also served on the computer-
science faculties of Purdue and Georgetown universities.

CATHERINE MEADOWS is a mathematician at the Naval Research Laboratory and a specialist in computer cryptography who has published several papers on
the subject.

JAMES ROSS owns Ross Engineering, Inc., a company
that specializes in devising countermeasures to computer
crime and technical surveillance. He has also taught electronics at West Point and at Capitol Institute of Technology in Maryland.

MILES SMID is manager of the Security and Speech Technology Group in the Institute for Computer Sciences and
Technology at the National Bureau of Standards. He is a
major contributor to the electronic funds transfer security
standards adopted by the U.S. Department of Treasury
and the American Banking Association.